Monks on Marriage

❧

MONKS ON MARRIAGE

A Twelfth-Century View

JEAN LECLERCQ, O.S.B.

THE SEABURY PRESS NEW YORK

1982
The Seabury Press
815 Second Avenue
New York, N.Y. 10017

Library of Congress Cataloging in Publication Data

Leclercq, Jean, 1911-
    Monks on marriage, a twelfth-century view.

    "Originated in a series of lectures given at Oxford University in the spring of 1979
and it is the natural continuation of a first series of lectures delivered in 1977 and now
published under the title, Monks and love in twelfth-century France [1979]"
—Introd.
    1. Marriage—Moral and religious aspects—Catholic Church—History—Addresses,
essays, lectures. 2. Love (Theology)—History of doctrines—Middle Ages,
600-1500—Addresses, essays, lectures. I. Title.

Bx2250.L383   1982   2618'358   81-13615
ISBN 0-8164-0507-7   AACR2

Contents

✣

INTRODUCTION

Purpose and Limits
of the Inquiry
❧

Today, fruitful studies shed light on various aspects of love in medieval times. We have, for example, studies on the family kinship, marriage as an institution, and the expression of love in mystical or secular literature. Profane writings frequently mention extramarital love, and this has already been studied to some extent. However, historians have neglected marital love literature. And it is this topic which I would like to discuss here. I shall attempt to do so in the light of a few manuscripts penned by monks and regular canons, men who chose to live a cloistral life of voluntary celibacy.

If I have selected the twelfth century for this inquiry, it is because this is a period of evolution in love literature. The texts written before that time tell us mainly about the conditions required for marriage: degrees of kinship, family interests, and legal consequences.[1] Kinship was considered to be more important than the two people concerned in the marriage. But in the twelfth century, the tide turned so to speak, and it was the union between the partners which primed rather than family alliances. With increasing evidence, we notice, stress is laid on the free choice and the mutual consent of the partners.[2] However, the canonical and the theological texts of those times were still principally concerned with the institutional aspect of the union of marriage, but we may lawfully ask, and it is interesting to do so, whether it is possible, over and beyond what the manuscripts tell us, to glimpse something of the sentimental, the affective side of the question: what do the texts reveal about the real human love between a man and his wife?

Chronicles and romances tell us about marriage in the aristocracy, in noble and knightly families. In a very fine book, G. Duby has discussed these medieval social weddings.[3] But what do we know about marriages between commoners? More texts than is generally thought provide an answer to this question, at least in part. Frequently such texts are found in the minor documents which have, on the whole, been less studied than the major ones. The elite minority of cultured laymen and clerics composed romances and poems in the vernacular or lyrical works in Latin while churchmen pored over the pastoral problems raised by the married state. But other writers, generally monks, wrote about marriage in a more spiritual vein. And these various categories of writers were constantly in touch with the worries and the joys of their married contemporaries. Thus, it occurred to me that it would be interesting and useful to confront in a first study some of these witnesses to the married life of real and ordinary people.[4]

This book originated in a series of lectures given at Oxford University in the spring of 1979 and it is the natural continuation of a first series of lectures delivered in 1977 and now published under the title *Monks and Love in Twelfth Century France.* I would like to seize the opportunity here of thanking Professor Michael Wallace-Hadrill, Professor Henry M.R.E. Mayr-Harting, and Dr. John Fenneley for having invited me to undertake this research.

My gratitude is due also to Sister Marie-Bernard Saïd, OSB, of the Abbaye d'Oriocourt, France, and Sister Mary Stephen of Saint Mary's Priory, Fernham, England, who have helped in the preparation of the manuscript; and to Father Jacques Winandy, OSB, who read the proofs.

Jean Leclercq
March, 1979

ONE

Love in Marriage as a Reality

❖

A Basic Fact: Marital Affection

It seems fitting to open our inquiry with the basic concept of marital affection because it is one which was at once traditional and universally accepted in the twelfth century. It is clearly expressed or at least implied in the majority of texts about marriage written by men of religion. It was studied by canonists[1] and theologians.[2] Marital love is a normal situation and is presupposed by spiritual writers. The implications of such love for the validity of marriage are now better recognized: without love there can be no marriage. Furthermore, it distinguishes the lawful wedded state from permanent cohabitation—which is not to be confused with isolated cases of adultery, occasional fornication, and concubinage—which, even if it is more or less permanent, is always irregular.[3] What interests us in the present juncture is not so much the legal consequences of the lawful married state as its essential element: true marital love between the partners. We do indeed notice that in many of the texts consulted marriage is considered solely as a social, legal, or sacramental fact. It implies, however, an affective element which, if we are to use the proper word, must be called love. Medieval canonical literature is more austere in tone than that of the fabliaux and romances, and it was possibly less widely read. However, it had its influence and is more revealing of the mentality which then prevailed than are the literary entertainments.

Canonical literature attributes much importance to that affective bond between two married people which is described as *affectio* or *affectus maritalis*. The attitude of a man towards his wife is called *uxoria affectio* or *affectus uxorius,* and the corresponding attitude of a woman towards her man is termed *affectio conjugalis,* which implies reciprocity of love. Such expressions were not the inventions of the Middle Ages: they were handed down from antiquity and are found in Roman law.[4] In ancient civilizations, as in the medieval traditions, a man was expected to dominate and to respect the woman he married, at least according to the letter of the law. And though marriages were sometimes "arranged" by the parents, this did not mean that love was absent. It was no more so then than it is today in non-Western civilizations where a man and woman do not always love each other before marriage though they may come to do so afterward. In the Middle Ages the development of postmarital love was often reciprocal. As early as the ninth century, Gauthier of Cologne wrote strongly about a lady that "She was united to her husband in faithfulness, affection, and love" (*suo viro fide, affectu ac dilectione sociata est*).[5]

The nature of conjugal love came to be more clearly defined in the twelfth century in parallel with the increasing stress laid by canonists on a woman's right to choose her husband.[6] According to their writings, steeped in the Christian culture and faith that was theirs, they acknowledged that love between married partners is a gift from God and that it implies first of all an element of grace. This must be accompanied by "a positive attitude that the partners must cultivate" with "a willingness to treat each other as a partner in marriage ought to be treated."[7] Thus, conjugal love is an "active love," one which should be a permanent attitude. There is also a "loving state of mind" which was a "dynamic attitude and was sufficient to constitute a valid marriage, without which, in fact, a marriage could not be said to exist."[8] Such love entails deep and affective attachment. This is the strong sense of the Latin words used: *afficere, affici.*[9] In the twelfth century, they are still sometimes considered as standing for one of the four passions of the soul defined by ancient philosophers. But more often they denote a movement of the "heart":[10] a form of *devotio* in the strongest sense of this word, implying the commitment of a man's whole being, an intense expression of fervor and ardor.[11] Gradually *affectus* and its derivations[12] came to be used more and more frequently. The first and most notable of the writers to use this word was Saint Bernard, and he did so in a way that was exemplary and determinative. In his sermons we find long and skillful variations on the form and content of the *affectus* experienced by "a heart afire with love" (*pectus amore calens*). Bernard warns that such a state of soul has something equivocal about it and must, therefore, be restrained by discretion (*discretio*), rightly oriented and conformed to order (*ordinatio*). This means that it must be controlled and occasionally tempered.[13] Once it has been thoroughly refined, such *affectus* inebriates the soul with love and leads it to cleave to God in transforming and deifying union (*sic affici deificari est*).[14] Love is the most exalted of the four affections weaving the bridgegroom's crown. And this especially when we love "all whom we should love," namely God because of his goodness and our neighbor by reason of the social connections established by our common human nature (*Deum amemus propter bonitatem et proximum propter naturae societatem*).[15] Wedded life is the primordial kind of community of nature and that is why Saint Bernard and other writers place marital love as one of the steps of the ladder of love culminating in union with God. The term *affectus caritatis,* applied to relations between married people, barely adds any fresh nuance to the already existing juridical notion handed down by tradition. The connection between charity and affection is always assumed but not always clearly mentioned. And it is because there can be no conjugal union without love that it became a metaphor of love for God.

Witness to Conjugality

Love between married persons was, then, held up by tradition as being the normal state of affairs. But it was also a reality proved by the texts. There are quite a number of indications, though they are dispersed, varied, and frequently vague, that makes them all the more worthy of attention.

The most frequent mentions of conjugal love are found in the charters, documents that can hardly be described as sentimental. Throughout the Middle Ages the manuscripts refer to "conjugal familiarity,"[16] or "conjugal love."[17] Often, when a donation was made to a wife during her lifetime, or in memory of her after her death, she is called the "most sweet one," "the most loved,"[18] or "lovable and very dear."[19] Sometimes a contract is made "because of a beloved wife."[20] In one cartulary we read that marriage is a "conjunction of love" contracted in the presence of a king.[21] Even though these short phrases might be mere stylistic clauses, they nevertheless show that love was assumed to exist between husband and wife. Furthermore, occasionally the sentiments expressed by such words are explicated and we read declarations like: "I have fallen in love with you, my dearest wife. I begged your hand from your parents and kinsfolk and they granted it to me. . . ."[22] Or again: "I desired to be united to you in the intimacy of marriage. And so I offer you this dowry out of love in honor of your sweetness and in view of the conjugal grace and the contract which joins us together."[23] In another cartulary we read: "Novilia, who are so dear to me and so loved, you the honest virgin who are going to be my wife, I, Ardengus, who offer you these gifts. . . ."[24] Another charter has: "To you, my most sweet and much loved wife, because of your looks and your beauty, I give you these gifts. . . ."[25] In this last instance, the words expressing the reasons for the gifts are taken from Psalm 44, a nuptial song which, together with the Song of Songs, another biblical love poem, was then frequently commented upon. Such effusiveness was not at all necessary for the acts to be valid. Thus we may assume that if husbands felt the urge to use such expressions in cartularies, they were something more than mere figures of speech.

The chronicles form another group of documents which occasionally testify to the existence of conjugal love. Some just make a passing mention of a "beloved wife,"[26] while others are more insistent. Interesting results have been obtained by the study of *The Ecclesiastical History,* the major work of Orderic Vital, a monk of Saint-Evroul.[27] It is evident from this work that though not all wives were happy in their marriage, many were both loving and loved. Frequently their love was put to the test by separation occasioned by war, the Crusades, or other circumstances beyond their control. Death brought about the final and lasting separation. And in this case, a wife's fidelity to her deceased husband was then proved by her remaining a widow, refusing to remarry. If there is any truth in the accounts given by romances of duels and tourneys, then mortal accidents were a frequent thing, and there must consequently have been a fair number of widows.

Love often remained faithful, too, even though husband and wife were separated by his absence from home. And thus *amor de longe* was a reality before becoming a literary theme. There were many occasions for separation in those days when "the Crusader baron left his wife and children alone for long years in the castle, and even sometimes his *lady* in a neighboring castle."[28] But the most usual and the most frequent case was for a Crusader to leave wife and children. In one Crusader chanson we can read a very realistic description of conjugal love: in the absence of her husband the wife, though she had other suitors, preferred to remain faithful to him (*Molt est fox qu'en veut parler.*)[29]

In this context historians quote the two letters dictated by Étienne de Blois and addressed to his wife Adèle during the first Crusade. He gives her news of the political and military events which keep him far from her. But he does so with a show of affection heightened by the ready pen of his chaplain. At the beginning and the end of each of his letters, we meet with expressions such as "my most gentle and loving wife. . ., my dearest one. . ., my beloved. . ., you whom I truly love. . ., my sweetest friend, my wife to whom I send all my best and most affectionate thoughts. . . ." One of the endings is most eloquent: "All this that, among other things I write to you, my dearest one, is very little, because I do not find words to say all that is in my heart, O my darling. . . . But as soon as possible, you will certainly see me back again. . . ."[30]

Iconography and the sculptures of the twelfth century also reflect the cloistral understanding of conjugal love. An example exists in the Church of the Cordeliers at Nancy. We see Adeline, countess of Vaudrémont, pressing to her bosom her husband, Hugh, whom she thought had been killed in the Holy Land from where he has finally returned after fifteen years or so. Romances frequently tell us that husband and wife mourned their deceased partner and were not to be consoled by any human love. Often, they decided to enter the monastic state.[31]

If recumbent effigies could speak, what marvelous love stories they would tell us! At least that is the impression we have from the pictorial illustration of the artists on funeral monuments. They all reflect something of the attitude to marriage inspiring many sculptors.

A recent study by Ilene H. Forsyth on *The Theme of Cockfighting in Burgundian Romanesque Sculpture* shows that many an ancient sarcophagus is embellished with the portrait of a deceased married couple united by conjugal love in death as in life, as well as with two fighting cocks. This may strike the modern mind as strange, but the image of friendly rivalry was used to represent love and counterlove and symbolized marriage: "true love always has the power of provoking love in return," and the cockfight evokes the "reciprocal passion of married couples, the completeness of their engagement to one another, a collaborative interplay between the partners, the unity of their mutual love." An example of this metaphor can be seen in the twelfth-century capital of the Abbey of Saulieu (and in other churches, some of which are monastic) in Burgundy, so deeply influenced by Cluny, Cîteaux and other cloisters where so many beautiful texts on marriage were written. The exegetical science of those times, especially as it was understood at Saint-Victor and other abbeys, helps to interpret these works of art which illustrate and ratify the theories exposed in literature.[32]

There exist many other minor witnesses to conjugality which it would be well worthwhile collating and studying. All that we can do within the limits of the present inquiry is to show the consideration they merit. Charters and chronicles hardly lend themselves to sentimental outpourings, and statues are dumb. However, they do have something to say, and the witness they bear is as credible as that contained in romances and spiritual writings. In their conciseness many passing allusions reveal esteem for the married state. We read, for example, in the chronicle of Bernold of Constance at the end of the eleventh century: "The seventh day of the Kalends of October, obit of Hugh, a married and most religious man. . . ."[33] And the cartulary of Würtemburg towards 1100 speaks of "marital chastity."[34] Later on another chronicler says even more clearly: "There are three ways in which a woman may be chaste: in conjugality, like Sarah and Suzanna; in widowhood, like Judith and Anna; in virginity like Mary."[35] It is touching that one of the proposed models of conjugality should be Suzanna, whose fidelity was, according to the Book of Daniel, so sorely put to the test.[36]

Defense of Conjugality

From the eleventh to the thirteenth century, and particularly throughout the twelfth, the traditionally recognized value of marriage with the faithful love it required and made possible was attacked by various people. Their contemporaries and some historians have called them Cathars, dualists, Manicheans. More recently they have been named, more or less precisely and correctly, the "heretics of the year

1000."[37] Over and beyond the differences of nomenclature, they all denied marriage to be good. As a result of their doctrines, a continuous line of defenders came to the fore to reaffirm the teaching and practice of the Church. One or two monastic witnesses will serve to exemplify the general trend.

About 1133–35, a certain William refuted Henry of Lausanne on this and many other points of doctrine. After having called to mind the three ends of marriage, one of which is legitimate love, and the three necessary conditions for validity, one of which is the "intention of the married partners to be faithful to each other unto death," William makes this important statement: "Marriage is constituted, not by the contract between two persons, but by an explicit agreement including the orientation of each life towards the other, and the love of the two people who legitimately love each other with an end to procreation." Thus, conjugal love and the intention to procreate are inseparable and neither the one nor the other is in itself sufficient to warrant union and its finality. There are three lawful reasons for dissolving marriage: impotence, which is an obstacle to procreation; "honest consent," for example for those who wish to enter the religious state; and fornication, which is a sure proof of the absence of true love.[38]

About ten years later, around the year 1144, Saint Bernard wrote against these heretics who denied marriage to be good. He took as his theme the verse in the Letter to the Hebrews (13: 4) which says: "Let marriage be held in honor among all, and let the marriage bed be undefiled."[39] To deny this, says Saint Bernard, would be to open the door to every form of libertinism, perversion, impurity. In other words, such a denial would authorize a shameful marriage rather than an honest one. But "marriage, which in itself is honest, cannot have been created dishonest by the author of all honesty." And honesty is not the privilege of a few volunteers for continence, it is also proper to married persons because marriage is the only state in which physical union is honest.

Marital union (*maritalis copula*) originates in the liberty to choose one's husband or wife (*libertas matrimonii*) from any walk of life. This same liberty authorizes a second and even a third marriage in those cases when one of the partners has died. It enables those who live a loose life of licentiousness to convert from a shameful union to an honest one.[40]

At the end of this treatise in the form of a sermon, Bernard sings the praises of the woman who has borne children, because she thus acquires the right to transmit the faith. He reminds us that Jesus himself praised the Canaanite woman for her faith and quotes in this connection Saint Paul's First Letter to Timothy (2: 15): "Woman will be saved if she continues in faith and good works."[41] Faith here, according to the original biblical text and theological tradition, is first of all conjugal fidelity. But in keeping with the context it is also the faith of the Church which a mother hands on to her children. This unique allusion to the fact of bearing children alludes not only to physical birth, but also to spiritual birth and growth. And so, in these various ways those who are unable or who do not wish to live a life of voluntary continence save their souls in and by marriage.

In the second half of the twelfth century, in answer to the attacks made by the Cathars against the stability of marriage, Egbert of Schönau (d. 1184) took up its defense and proved the lasting nature of the union of hearts (*unitas mentium*) set up by the marriage contract (*foedus conjugale*). Even though the two partners should separate in order to enter a monastery, the marital tie remains. And Egbert adds, addressing the Cathars, "We do not advise this sort of separation to anyone, as you do."[42] Like so many other writers, he repeats that the only real justification for divorce is adultery, implying unfaithfulness in love (*sola fornicationis causa divortium fieri potest*).[43] He too legitimates "the work of marriage" (*opus conjugale*) because, he says, human beings are not made of iron (*non. . . tam ferreos esse*):[44] what is allowed cannot be evil (*et quia licitum est, malum non est*).[45] It is even a duty (*officium conjugii*),[46] a debt. It is here that the notion of a due (*debitum*) transforms the marriage act into something worthy of justice and charity, and free from sin. He repeats "it is never a sin."[47] Egbert evokes very discreetly the temperance and reserve a husband should show towards his wife in physical love and so respect God in her. He goes on to say that a man of good sense should know all about this[48] and that it is not his business as a preacher to go into details but merely to propose an ideal.

He then explains with a certain accuracy the "indulgence" which God and the Church accord to the marriage act. The word *indulgence* (*venia*) does not mean here pardon or absolution, but rather a concession. Things of lesser importance are conceded in view of higher and better things.[49] Consequently, if fleshly pleasure should go beyond reasonable limits, there might be something slightly sinful in it (*aliquid peccati*). But any such trace of sin is only a minor one excused by the good which results from marriage. In the same way the pleasure a man has in eating must be justified by the end, the intention to nourish the body. All this is distinctly a different matter from major faults such as murder. Egbert pushes this principle to extremes. Congress in marriage without the intention of begetting children and for the sole purposes of sexual pleasure is in itself a sin, though the sin is only venial: it is excused by the other benefits of marriage and is the object of an indulgence, a permission. It is allowed so that the greater evil of fornication might be avoided.[50] It is interesting that Egbert, who also described the mystical experiences of his sister Elisabeth, should write long pages in defense and illustration of conjugal love. Of all anti-catharist literature of those times, Egbert's work is one of the most elaborate.

TWO

Conjugal Love as a Doctrinal Issue

Life Situations

Conjugal love, though it was a firmly established fact, nevertheless sometimes met with difficulties arising from social situations or the legacy of the past. Medieval society set up social barriers between the men and women of the different categories or "orders" within which it was then lawful to marry. There were two such orders: that composed of warriors, knights, and nobles of all ranks, whose vocation it was to fight, and that made up of the peasants and the city people, whose vocation it was to work in some way. A third category comprised clerics and religious, whose vocation it was to pray and who were, naturally enough, excluded from marriage. This triple class system existed before the twelfth century, but during the course of the century it became even more complex, particularly in the order of the warriors. This social distinction arose during feudal times. According to certain historians it had died out or at least was on the point of doing so. But we find it clearly attested by many documents even after the close of the twelfth century. The social barrier system became more complicated between nobles and roturiers, that is, between people of higher and lower social rank. For many there was absolutely no question of freedom to choose one's partner. Parents frequently arranged the marriage of their teenage children, particularly their daughters, and this was quite a common thing even in the middle class. Marriages between serfs were controlled by the lords and masters.

Moreover, in certain regions, the practice of primogeniture in the aristocratic classes and even in other classes sought to manipulate the distribution of the family estates and assure progeny. Thus, in many cases only the eldest son could marry. This entailed two consequences: first, many marriages were arranged by the parents of the fiancée for political or financial reasons. Secondly, a certain number of men and women found themselves condemned to involuntary celibacy. It is possible that other sociological data were involved here too, but at least from this very brief sketch, we can already picture certain aspects of twelfth-century society.

The married state with the lovemaking it implied was, then, the normal state, not only in the sense that it was in conformity to the norm preached by Christian morality, but also because it was the most frequent form of union. The freedom with which people contracted marriage had limits, but can it be said that these limits excluded love? We have no reason to assume that marriages in the twelfth century were loveless. There was not only sexual gratification but affection as well. But what is specifically characteristic of the twelfth century is that love became more explicit than in previous times: what had long been a *praxis* became a *theoria*. This did not happen easily, hindered as it was by certain cultural elements inherited from the past.

The Church has always asserted the goodness of marriage, and one of her representatives who, on this question, had the greatest influence during the Middle Ages was Saint Augustine. From the very first line of his treatise, of which the title is characteristic, *The Good of Marriage,* he situates the family institution in a very broad perspective, according to which man has been created "sociable" and made for "friendship." As Augustine says:

> Since every man is a part of the human race, and human nature is something *social* and possesses the capacity of *friendship* as a great and natural good, for this reason God wished to create all men from one, so that they might be held together in their *society,* not only by similarity of race, but also by the bond of blood relationship. And so it is that the first natural tie of human *society* is man and wife. Even these God did not create separately and join them as if strangers, but He made the one from the other, indicating also the power of union in the side from whence she was drawn and formed. They are joined to each other side by side who walk together and observe together where they are walking. A consequence is the union of *society* in the children. . . .[1]

Augustine has shown in many other texts how the matrimonial life is a way of anticipating this universal friendship, this "friendly society" which will be the City of God. However, he could not help expressing some reservations as to the sanctifying value of marriage, and this for many reasons, among which was the memory of his faithful, but unlawful union with his concubine—a union for which his mother Monica had reproached him and which delayed his conversion. Certain ideas, commonly admitted at that time, contributed also to his reticence about marriage. Among other theories, not only was original sin transmitted in procreation, but that virginity is a higher state than marriage. Greek thought also had its influence, and according to a particular Greek aesthetic conception, the number of the elect preordained by God had been reached, and thus it was no longer necessary to propagate the human race. It was considered, too, that the passionate movement of human nature restrains the full possession and operation of reason. In brief, marital love bore the mark of a certain guilt, which though it was the object of indulgence (*venia*) and "excused" by the good of marriage, inevitably influenced the mentality of the time.[2]

Another Father of the Church, Saint Jerome, had also recognized the good of marriage, but since he had to refute Jovinian, who denied the value of virginity, he insisted so much on the worth of this state that the honor of marriage seemed to be devalued.[3] This cultural and religious heritage was complex, and though it was only vaguely known to Christians, it cast over the love activity a certain suspicion. It was felt that marriage was good, *but* not entirely so. And it was the *but* which played such an important part. Of course, the positive value of marriage was not forgotten, even during the period of rigorism which was that of Gregorian reform. An austere but human hermit, Peter Damian, wrote most magnificently on "the mystery of brotherly love" which "unites the minds and the bodies of married poeple." He explains that the end of the marriage is to make possible such "burning love."[4] Nevertheless, a certain uneasiness subsisted in many a conscience. Added to this, the external guarantee or sanction given to marriage by public formalities had not yet been universally acknowledged as necessary. However, a secret, "clandestine" marriage always implied lifelong fidelity to one's partner. But human fickleness often profited by the fact that there had been no witnesses to the mutual consent exchanged in private. This gave rise to many problems of the psychological, spiritual, and juridical order of things. Such, in brief, was the situation at the beginning of the twelfth century.

Pastoral Concerns

Little by little, these problems became matter for reflection by married Christians and this in direct proportion to the economic and cultural development of society as a whole. The cathedral schools in towns and cities recruited more and more clerics. In the course of their studies, they came into contact with matrimonial problems either through their masters who were concerned with pastoral care or else in preparation for their own activity in this field. Many of the "sentences"—short formulas borrowed from Scripture or from Tradition—brought up for discussion by the schoolmen concerned marriage and dealt with the joys and sorrows of the matrimonial state, conjugal love, the transmission of original sin in procreation and its consequences, the temptations and faults affecting the marital relations, and all the sexual problems suggested not only by Old Testament and patristic writings, but also by life situations.

In this connection it has been said that these questions were the "urgent and deeply felt anxieties of mature and serious people." Such modern terminology is not found in the sentences, but we do find its equivalent. Frequently there is mention of "questions arising from the doubts of certain people"[5] on this or that point. And it even happens that we read of a sort of counseling session, as for example, in the treatise by Hugh of Saint-Victor *On the Sacraments*. In one of the chapters, he discusses the case of a man who has contracted two successive marriages, one clandestinely and the other in front of witnesses.[6] The private marriage had been contracted without formality or witnesses, "as is sometimes done," remarks Hugh. Later, the husband "repents" and contracts a second marriage, this time a public one. Each of his wives claims, as by right, the poor man's fidelity. He wishes to disavow his first marriage but fails to prove that it is not valid. And "So", says Hugh, "You come to ask me for counseling." He can do no more than remind his client of the Church's law and teaching. Both are quite complex and give no practical details as to the cases when a marriage is considered to be valid. A long dialogue between the unfortunate husband and the counselor ensues during which they attempt to clarify the situation. The whole matter is one of a "scruple of conscience" and the client is asking for a "counsel of salvation." The counselor too has his conscience, his heart which dictates his answers. All that he can do is to remind his client of the Church's teaching and help him to find a solution to a conflict in which he and God alone are the only fitting judges as to motivations and circumstances. Under the stress of his emotion, the husband speaks aloud to God, exposing his unhappy state, begging for forgiveness if he has sinned, and asking what he should do by way of reparation. The counseling session ends with a long and moving prayer.

This is only one among many other similar texts and they all go to prove that the concern was not merely one of speculative teaching or academic discussion, but of giving practical advice in vital questions. The doctrine on marriage is thus elaborated in the crucible of life situations. The major concern is always to restate that marriage is first of all a matter of love, on condition that this is taken in its primitive and purest sense of charity, expressed in conjugal affection. This includes "ardent and persevering charity with fidelity unto death," protection and union for the purpose of begetting children. The texts contain innumerable Latin formulas which are pregnant expressions of the true content of marriage, a life of love between persons in love: "love is the delectation of the heart," "love is mutually and freely chosen (*dilectio*)."

This conviction that marriage is a life of love is expressed too in marriage rituals which began to be drawn up in order to palliate the inconveniences of clandestine marriage. The presence of a priest was required and the ceremonial was drafted in such way as to bring out the symbolism of the mystery contained in the sacrament. The liturgy ratified what had hitherto been a mere exchange of verbal consent. It is stipulated in the rituals that "there must be love"; "if there is love between them, let them be united. . . ." Prayers are said so that the wedded man and wife "always have for one another the mutual love of the grace of the married state," a concord by which they become equals and that they may have for one another "a same freely chosen love (*dilectio*)."[8] Thus, paradoxically, even the ritualization of marriage through external ceremonies and words helped to personalize and internalize conjugal union.

We may possibly wonder whether in practice throughout the twelfth century, everyone poor and rich, villeins, burghers, and nobles alike, contracted marriage in keeping with all these formalities. This cannot be proved, but the texts of rituals show us the general ideal proposed to all. Often the wedding ceremony began in the church porch, and then after going into the sanctuary the sacrament of marriage was associated with that of the Eucharist. More and more, and by every possible means, conjugal union was consciously and publicly recognized as an integral part of Christian living.

Theological Solutions

Parallel with this effort made in the domain of pastoral and liturgy, a similar move forward was made in the reflection of theologians whose main task was to reconcile the different facts related in the texts handed down by tradition. Such texts, though often beautiful and always abundant, were occasionally divergent in the ideas they expressed, for reasons which have been already discussed here. An attempt was made in the first generation of the twelfth-century writers by two masters in pastoral matters, Anselm and Raoul of Laon. They trained clerics in the town schools to help the faithful solve their various difficulties, including matrimonial ones. The same goals were pursued later in the century at Paris by theologians such as Hugh of Saint-Victor and Peter Lombard, and then almost everywhere in the schools by canonists such as Yvo of Chartres and Gratian. This teaching has been the subject matter of such literature and thus it will be sufficient merely to mention lesser-known witnesses or those who have but recently been studied. We have for example, at the opening of the twelfth century, *Magister A,* who seems to be a certain Elmer of Canterbury whose *Sentences* were published in 1974 by Heinrich Rheinhardt. Like his contemporaries of Laon and the other town schools, *Magister A* considers marriage a positive state of life. More than a remedy for man's sinful propension, it is a means of salvation. It gives man the opportunity of restoring the "order of charity," that blissful state of mind in which Adam, waking from his deep sleep during which Eve was drawn out of his side, cried out in love and thus "announced prophetically the predilection and the state of life which should exist between man and woman."[9] By his insistence on love, Elmer quickened the motivations of certain articles in matrimonial law, such as the prohibition to marry kinsfolk, for, he says, marriage should extend love to others beyond the family circle whose members we love because of blood ties.[10] We do not find any such thought in the treatise written by Bonizon of Sutri in the preceding century.[11]

Theorists were sometimes more original in their speculations on the Trinity, the Incarnation, the Redemption and on sin and grace than they were when they dealt with marriage. Abelard is a good example of this. Though he was such a creative and vigorous theologian in other subjects, he does not seem to have made any outstanding or original contribution to the doctrine on marriage. At least so it would seem if we judge from his texts as they have so far been published.[12] There is nothing on marriage in the two recently edited volumes of his *Theologia.* In his *Sic et Non,* he does no more than propose the facts for and against marriage as they are to be found in the traditional patristic writings. And he insists mainly on the negative facts. In the chapter on marriage his main reference is Saint Jerome. Abelard draws no conclusions,[13] he simply exposes the question and presents a *dossier sans conclusion*—a dossier without conclusion[14]—which is more confusing than enlightening. As was pointed out earlier on, this "yes, but" in connection with marriage emphasizes the "but" more than the "yes." Like Augustine, who had guilty memories about his concubine, so Abelard was haunted by memories of his love affair with Héloïse. In character and thought Abelard was closer to Jerome than to Augustine, and it was Jerome who exerted the greater influence on him. Jerome himself had been influenced by Christian teaching, of course, but also by certain pagan moralists, especially the Stoics, whose attitude to sexuality was negative. These various factors affected on the one hand Abelard's teaching, and on the other, the attitude of Héloïse when she refused to marry him.[15] A complete study of Abelard's teaching on love based on a broader basis than his correspondence with Héloïse would doubtless show to what extent his personal experience impeded his consistency as a theologian. Nevertheless, in the *Epitome* redacted by one of his disciples, he is said to have quoted a definition of marriage which states that husband and wife "may have intercourse without sin" (*licet eis sine culpa commisceri*).[16]

In his recently published *Sentences,* Gilbert de la Porrée (d. 1154) also deals with the matrimonial problems arising from life situations such as the fact of a man "repenting" after clandestine marriage and contracting a public one, or the situation created when one of the partners consents that the other take vows and enter the religious life. Contradictory opinions among the Fathers of the Church sometimes oblige a stand to be taken for one or the other of divergent opinions. Solutions to the problems are sought in the "judgment of the Church" and in common practice. Even the authority of Saint Augustine has to cede before the current *praxis* because, as it is written, "The Church no longer holds that opinion" (*Sed modo non tenet ecclesia*). Common sense is the final reference. The last sentence of Gilbert's chapter on marriage ends like a manifesto of freedom: "Augustine states that it is possible to contract a good marriage after having known bad union in adultery. Leo says the opposite. Answer: Augustine states the truth; Leo seeks to frighten us because of the consequences. We must remember what Saint Paul says: 'Let a woman marry whom she will,' which is to be understood as meaning that we must discover what she wants in order to know if she wishes to marry, but we must also examine whether the man she wants to marry also wishes to marry."[17]

These efforts resulted, at the end of the century, in anthologies such as the *London Questions* summarizing the thought of preceding generations. James A. Brundage has shown that the matters dealt with reply to the practical concerns of the Christian conscience.[18] The contributions made by pastoral theological, canonical, and liturgical research may be recapitulated in two major points: first, that marriage is a free consent between two partners. It is most primarily a contract, in the legal sense of the word, but a free and mutual acceptance. Union in the consummation of marriage is subordinated to this acceptance. It is not sexual congress which characterizes marriage, but love. And love consists in the conviviality of conjugal affection in the sense which has already been defined. However, such consent and affection are normally proved by physical union, which, so to speak, puts a seal upon them. Consent supposes liberty: the freedom to marry or not to marry, and freedom to choose one's partner. Recent studies have shown that this was probably the greatest acquisition in things matrimonial during the twelfth century.[19] This does not mean, however, that in every instance practice conformed to theory. But law and theology guaranteed freedom of consent. Examples to be quoted further on will show that where this free consent is lacking, a public marriage contracted under pressure could be declared invalid. To prove that it is free consent alone which constitutes marriage, consummation was occasionally delayed for a day or two.

The second point is that the acquisition of the right to freedom of choice in marriage went parallel with that of the liberty to enter a monastery, or not to do so, and also to go to the monastery of one's own choosing.[20] Furthermore, it seems that the desire to enter the monastic life after having contracted lawful marriage by mutual consent was quite often a legitimate reason for separation provided that there was again mutual consent.[21] History records the names of married partners one or both of whom entered the monastery. And we even have the record of a speech made by Ansold de Maule to his wife Odeline in such circumstances.[22] Orderic Vital narrates the facts in these terms: "After having spent fifty-three years in knighthood and come to old age, he began to feel unwell and remained in this state for seven weeks. . . ." Though he did not have to stay in bed, he felt that death was close at hand, so he asked the monks of Saint Evroul to take him as one of them so that he might die a monk. It was frequent in those days for a man or a woman to ask to be clothed with the habit *ad succurrendum,* in the belief that they would thus get to heaven with special help.[23] Ansold explained to the monks that he no longer felt bound to show protection (*pietas*) towards his wife and children. Thus, the Community accepted him. After giving his last words of advice to his eldest son, he addressed his wife in the following words: "My dear sister and beloved wife Odeline, listen kindly now to my request. Hitherto we have been faithful to one another in lawful marriage. By the grace of God we have lived together without difference or shameful dispute for more than twenty years. We have begotten legitimate progeny by our lawful union. . . ." The opening words of this speech might well have been inspired by the words of the Song of Songs, "My sister, my bride," and the continuation of the speech resembles more that of a monk than of a knight. Further on in the narrative Orderic, in connection with Ansold's approaching union with the earth in death, puts into his mouth the words used by Saint Paul when he speaks of the duty of married persons to pay each other their due (*debitum persolvere*). Ansold then asks his wife's permission to become a monk and "to receive the habit of our holy Father Benedict, even though it be black." These last words are later explained by a quotation from the Song, "I am black but beautiful," and by the traditional interpretation by which *black* signifies human wretchedness and *beauty* the Christian's dignity.

This speech goes to show, at least, that Orderic considered Ansold always to have loved his wife and still to do so. She loved him too: "This good woman who had made a habit of never thwarting his will shed many tears. . . . But, obedient to her husband, as was her custom, she assented to his request." Ansold died three days later. But his wife had mourned him already because they were separated in their old age, after a long life of fidelity in marriage. It must be noticed that Ansold separated from his wife to enter the monastery only after she had given her consent, just as they had been joined in marriage by mutual consent.

There were, of course, still some unhappy married people whose emotions were sung by writers of "songs of unhappy wives."[24] But this does not necessarily mean that the cause of unhappiness was the lack of initial consent. The difficult questions which were the object of so much literature were dealt with on the level of canon law by matrimonial suits which will be discussed further on.[25] In such lawsuits, Church institutions attempted to remedy difficult situations by reconciling the partners with one another as far as possible. In assuring the prerequisite freedom of choice in marriage, the Church aimed at forestalling broken marriages. Unfortunately, she was not always successful in this, but at least forced marriages were, in principle, precluded. In the second half of the twelfth century, religious organizations—Cathedral chapters and abbeys—allowed men and women residing on their properties to choose a partner for marriage dependent on other masters and lords. In this way, the right recognized by the Church was allowed to peasants in rural communities and not restricted to nobles in castles.[26]

In cohabitation, union is a debt which each partner owes to the other and which was freely contracted at the time of marriage. To give the conjugal rights, as Saint Paul points out, is a duty of strict justice and, consequently, an occasion for merit.[27] Saint Augustine in his day wrote that the result of such union should be to prepare new citizens for the City of God. In this sense, marriage was a *seminarium civitatis,* "a seedbed of the City." In the twelfth century, Gratian and others modified this formula in a very significant way. It became *seminarium caritatis,* "a seedbed of charity," thus showing that matrimonial union is meant to serve charity.[28]

In connection with the pleasure accompanying lovemaking, the formulas used by canonists and theologians vary. Some, misinterpreting the word *venia,* which for Saint Augustine means indulgence, say that the marriage act is accompanied by sin, but that it is only venial and is to be looked upon with indulgence and "excused" by the "good of marriage." This, finally, means that there is no sin at all. Other canonists and theologians, however, assert bluntly that there is no fault. Towards the middle of the tenth century, Ratherius of Verona wrote, "There are two sorts of marital union, one faultless, the other accompanied with venial fault."[29] Towards the beginning of the next century, Theitmar of Mersebourg, speaking to laymen, said, "May those who are married in Christ be allowed to live in all innocence...."[30] In the twelfth century, Robert of Melun stated clearly, "Union in the flesh between a man and a woman would be a sin were they not married."[31] Thus, fleshly union is not sinful within the married state. There is no mention in these texts of the intention of procreation. Probably the clearest evidence to the absence of sin and the meritorious nature of matrimonial union is the text in which Saint Bernard explains to monks the different degrees of obligation of certain laws both in the monastic and the married state. "There are certain acts which merit glory when performed, but which can be omitted without fault. Consequently, if they are done they are fittingly rewarded, but if they are not done, there is no punishment. For instance, it is no little virtue not to touch a woman, but if a man embrace his own wife there is surely no fault in it."[32]

Pleasure accompanying marital relations must be used with moderation and temperance by which each partner practices self-control and a certain restraint in regard to the other. It might be wondered whether the texts mentioning temperance in marriage allude simply to the marriage act itself, which, properly speaking, is not subordinate to reason to the same extent as other human acts. Reading about Abelard's exclusive obsession with Héloïse and of Erec's passion for Enide, one would tend to think that it is a man's whole conduct which should be controlled by reason in order that he be free to go about his daily duties: study for Abelard, deeds of knightly valor for Erec.[33] It has been pointed out that the code of courtly love—when and if ever it was observed—enjoined restraints which were just as exacting as those of Christian morals.[34]

These newly acquired dispositions in the theory of marriage presuppose that man and woman are equal in their nature as humans and in their dignity as Christians and this because they are both made in the image of God. This was commonly held and taught throughout the twelfth century by the masters of the school of Laon and elsewhere. There may be, they say, inferiority of function for a woman, but this must not be exaggerated: it is in some way similar to the inferiority of the Son who, as man, states that the Father is greater than he, whereas they are equals as to their divinity.[35] There are exceptions to this common doctrine. Abelard's teaching was one such exception. But it was "erroneous, and shows that the lover of Héloïse was less of a feminist than the majority of spiritual writers."[36] This is certainly true for his theological works. But in his letters to Heloïse where he draws up a rule for nuns, he constantly stresses the privileged role played by women in the Old and the New Testament and in the primitive Church. And this, he says, is a role they can still play.[37] The antifeminist tirade of his *Lament over Samson,* who fell victim to Delilah, as other men had fallen into the clutches of other women, can be given an optimistic interpretation. According to Peter Dronke, Abelard used irony to suggest the contrary of what he actually said.[38] On the whole, secular poets were more severe on women than were theologians and spiritual writers. Possibly the churchmen, meditating and respecting the teaching of the Church, tended to be less excessive in their writings than the more passionate secular authors, who sometimes did no more than conform to satirical themes borrowed from pre-Christian literature.[39]

To conclude, we may say that though twelfth-century theologians, canonists, and spiritual writers discuss marriage, they do not say much about its connection with love. They state the objective norms which married couples are expected to assume in their spiritual life. They point out that there is in marriage an element of mystery, beyond human comprehension, and that though disappointment is always possible, there is also a genuine chance for deep happiness. In spite of its equivocal nature, stressed by twelfth-century authors, the basic elements of marriage, considered as being a form of Christian living, were henceforth clearly defined and accorded. It was now an acquired fact that married love cannot be reduced to sensual pleasure, for it is very much greater and it uplifts the marriage act to its own high level.

Such was the official teaching in the twelfth century. To what extent did it reach the man in the street? It originated in the pastoral concerns of the clergy and was developed by masters of patristic sentences, by theologians and canonists. Gradually it came out of the schools and seeped into the conscience of the faithful with further psychological niceties. This happened principally during confession, a practice which became more and more general from the end of the twelfth century onward. M. Sheehan quotes a moving passage from the *Summa for Confessors* written by Thomas of Chobham between the years 1210 and 1216. Wives are invited to profit by the moments of most intimate union (*in cubiculo et inter medios amplexus*) in order to preach good caressingly (*blande*) to their husbands because it is during such moments that a woman can "soften the heart of her husband" (*cor viri emollire*). Similar advice is given to husbands. We have here charity in the form of matrimonial pastoral or, as we would say today, the apostolate of married couples, incorporated into the very act of marriage by which they become one flesh. This *Summa* has come down to us and "more than one hundred manuscripts remain. Many of them can be shown to have been used in priories and colleges where they would have been accessible to a larger readership. . . ."[40] And this was only one of the handbooks for confessors minting, so to speak, the "new ideas" on marriage which were the fruit of several generations of research and thinking. Such manuals made these theories "directly available to the priest at the parish level and to his parishioners in a most explicit way. . . . For northwest Europe at least, it is clear that, by the end of the twelfth century, the new ideas on marriage were being taught."[41]

THREE

Spiritual Content of Marital Love

✣

The Witness of Hugh of Saint-Victor

The authors of sentences and the canonists generally confined themselves to stating that marriage is a good thing and that it cannot exist without love. Such were the dry bones of the facts, and it was left to writers more directly interested in a deep spiritual life and the connected questions of religious psychology to explicate the contents of these realities. The surest way of illustrating this is to make a thorough analysis of a few witnesses brought forward in chronological order. The value of such a demonstration necessarily lies not only in the aptness of their images and ideas, but also in the precision of their terminology. Let it be said, once and for all, that it must neither shock nor surprise us that spiritual men should use, with no trace of either complacency or repression, a distinctly realistic language contrasting with the manner of speech of more recent periods.

Between 1131 and 1141, Hugh of Saint-Victor, who contributed to the working out of practical pastoral solutions and theological doctrine, also wrote at length on the psychological and spiritual human contents of conjugal union. He did so in a letter which was in fact a treatise addressed to a bishop who had consulted him *On the Virginity of the Blessed Virgin Mary*.[1] He shows how her espousal illustrates perfectly that marriage is contracted by consent and not by consummation. Saint Luke tells us that Mary consented freely to marry Joseph, after she had talked the matter over with God's messenger and received all the necessary information, in particular, the answer to an objection which seemed to be insurmountable. Hugh comments at length on this dialogue between Mary and God, through the intermediary the angel Gabriel.[2] Mary's consent to marriage was clearly not consent to either consummation or to the obligation to pay the marriage rights. Union in the flesh is the normal consequence, the companion (*comes*), the function (*officium*) and not the good of marriage in itself.[3] As this exceptional marriage shows, the important and sufficient element is the *societas*, community of life, cohabitation; the engagement taken by each partner to seek no other society, by the anticipated refusal of adultery. Briefly, marriage is the good of charity. If marriage can be described as holy when it is accompanied with the ardor of the union in which the two become one flesh, it certainly can be said to be so in the absence of any such union. This leads Hugh to describe at length the total content of marital love:

> Can you find anything else in marriage except conjugal society which makes it sacred and by which you can assert that it is holy? And if this is true when the two become one flesh, is it not even more so when they become one mind? If they make each other partner of their flesh and are holy, is it possible for them to be partners in the soul and not be holy? Far be it! "The two shall become one flesh. This mystery is a profound one, it refers to Christ and the Church" (Eph. 5:31–32). The two shall become one soul. This is a great mystery, it refers to God and the soul. See now the nature of the contract by which they bind themselves in consented marriage. Henceforth and forever, each shall be to the other as a same self in all sincere love, all careful solicitude, every kindness of affection, in constant compassion, unflagging consolation, and faithful devotedness. And this in such a way that each shall assist the other as being one's own self in every good or evil tiding, the companion and partner of consolation, thus proving that they are united in trial and tribulation. Finally, each one shall attend outwardly to the needs of the other's body, taking it to self as being his own flesh to cherish, and so shall he also attend inwardly to love for the heart, as though it were his own soul to keep in peace and quiet (as far as lies within him) without worry. In this way they shall dwell in the peace of a holy society and the communion of a sweet repose so that it no longer be the one who lives, but the other. Thus each shall live for self even more happily and blessedly. Such are the good things of marriage and the happiness of the chaste society of those who love each other.[4]

However, immediately an objection springs to the mind. According to the Augustinian school of thought, the principal end of marriage is the begetting of children. Hugh raises this point and states with reinforced clarity the exact nature of the love implied by matrimonial consent. The pivotal text for this demonstration comes from the Book of Genesis and is quoted by Christ in the Gospel: "A man shall leave his father and mother and be joined to his wife, and the two shall become one."[5] In this verse the important word is in Latin, *adhaerere,* which signifies to be joined to, to be united with. Hugh uses this word several times and clearly explains its meaning: "Does this joining mean only sexual union?" he asks. No! it entails three facts: cohabitation, freely chosen love (*dilectio*), commixture. Such is the exclusive and unique "society" common to both partners (*societas singularis*), in which each must give self to the other and in view of which a man prefers the single (*singularis*) affection for his wife (*affectus uxoris*) to the love for his father and mother. Thus the "joining" mentioned by Hugh means also the affection of the heart and the bond of love by which man and wife live together (*de affectu cordis et vinculo socialis dilectionis*). It is easy to recognize under these words Saint Augustine's teaching on marriage as a *societas amicalis,* a friendly society.

Little by little the stress shifts from "union" to "love." It is this love, already inferred by the free choice, the election of a partner, which is the source of marital happiness. This is conjugal love taken in its richest meaning and not merely union in the flesh—which is only one aspect—and it is this which is the sacrament, which is the sign and symbol as well as the means of its effective realization, of the great mystery of the union between Christ and the Church. Several vigorous formulas insist upon the primacy of love: the indivisible embrace of love (*individuus amoris nexus*); the equality of an only love (*singularis dilectionis parilitas*); the everlasting bond in love (*individua semper dilectione sociari*).[6] It would be possible to compose an entire litany of conjugal love with phrases taken from these pages. Hugh has no difficulty in showing that all this applies to Mary and Joseph as to all Christian married people. At the end of his treatise, such praise of the primacy of love as necessary and sufficient to the initial consent is taken up again and applied to the various psychological nuances of the conjugal love of a man for his wife, for whom he feels a certain pity and natural compassion. The wife allows herself to be loved by her husband because of a certain need arising from her state (*necessitate conditionis*), she herself being "admitted by natural kindness to this society of love."[7]

Hugh of Saint-Victor insists on the specific nature of love in each partner, as is only normal considering the differences of sex. He ends his letter with words taken from the greatest of love songs, the Song of Songs itself. This nuptial song sings of conjugal love,[8] and, says Hugh, God found no other human affection which so aptly describes the love of the divine Word for the Church and for each single member. This biblical expression of love enabled man to taste inwardly in his heart a great mystery which had been hidden from him from all ages. Only through the analogy of conjugal love could the human mind grasp something of so great a mystery.

The Surprising Richard of Saint-Victor

Another and still more surprising cloistral writer who witnessed to conjugal love is Richard of Saint-Victor. Though many authors tended to idealize married life, they were not blind to the difficulties inherent in this state and which are simply consequences of the basic principles these writers taught. Marriage requires consent and this presupposes love: a partner is freely chosen because he is loved or so that he or she might come to be loved. Throughout married life, consent and love are mutually conditional to the point of being almost identical. This does not mean that with the passing of time, love freely chosen and even, perhaps, the initial consent are not put to the test. Certain courtly romances describe instances of consent in which there was neither free choice nor love. In such cases satisfaction in love is sought in adultery and this is presented as being something good. Monastic authors are fully aware that marital love and fidelity are subject to periods of crisis. On a high literary level, Richard of Saint-Victor (d. 1173) discusses some of these difficulties with a surprising psychological insight.

He first describes, in striking lyrical terms, love between man and wife in a treatise entitled *Of the Four Degrees of Passionate Love*. The theme of this work is the wound of love and the consequent sickness of love which is a commonplace in all love literature. In the Jewish and the Christian tradition, the wound of love is the major theme of the

Song of Songs[9] and the texts it inspired. Richard, having introduced his theme, exults with joy at the prospect of singing the praise of love. Saint Bernard of Clairvaux, in the first of his *Sermons on the Song,* also exults in a similar way. Richard, after his first effusions, goes on to intone an ardent hymn to love personified: "O vehemence of love! O thou violence of charity. . . ." In the first lines of his treatise we find expressions similar to those of courtly literature:

> I am wounded by love. Love urges me to speak of love. Gladly do I give myself up to the service of love and it is sweet and altogether lovely to speak about love. This is a joyful subject and very fruitful; one that will not weary the writer or fatigue the reader. For that which savors of charity pleases the heart's taste beyond measure. "If a man would give all the substance of his house for love, it would utterly be condemned."[10] Great is the power of love, wonderful the virtue of charity.[11]

In this treatise, Richard follows the fashion of thought and literary expression common to practically all love literature but used more especially in the twelfth century in the treatises and poems of courtly love. In nearly all these writings, it is interesting to notice, we find that love is attributed different steps or degrees, the number of which varies from one author to another. Richard of Saint-Victor, as we gather from the title he gives to his treatise, distinguishes various degrees. Before applying this distinction to love for God, he gives a psychological analysis of each step. It is the first which interests us in the context of this study. Richard writes that in human affections the first degree is good, and he goes on:

> We know that among human affections conjugal love must take the first place, and therefore in wedded life that degree of love which generally dominates all other affections seems to be good. For the mutual affection of intimate love draws closer the bonds of peace between those who are pledged to each other, and make that indissoluble, life-long association pleasant and happy.[12]

How, we may ask, does this degree of love manifest itself? Richard describes it in magnificent terms:

> But let us return to that degree of love which we first mentioned

and called "wounded love." Do you not feel as if sometimes you were shot through the heart when the fiery dart of this love penetrates the inmost mind of man, pierces his affections so that he can in no way contain or hide the burning of his desire. He burns with desire, his affections are stirred, he is in fever and gasps, sighing deeply and drawing long breaths. These are certain signs of a wounded soul, groans and sighs, a pale and averted face. But this degree sometimes affords some respite and allows for the cares and anxieties of necessary business. After the manner of feverish men who are troubled by this illness, sometimes they burn more fiercely, then by attending to their affairs they feel some relief. But after a short interval they burn again, greater heat supervenes, and the broken spirit is once more set on fire and burns more fiercely. Thus the fever of love, often waning but always returning more acutely, gradually weakens the spirit, wears down and exhausts the strength until it completely conquers the soul and lays it low. It occupies the soul wholly with thoughts about itself, engrosses and controls it wholly so that it cannot tear itself away or consider anything else.[13]

Elsewhere he writes that this love "fastens the mind indissolubly by not allowing it to move over to other concerns" and "it often takes away a man's attention and his foresight from providing and disposing things suitably."[14] We may wonder whether it was not this violent, ardent, and obsessional love that makes a man incapable of giving his mind to any other occupation and concern which beset Abelard in his relation with Héloïse—if we are to believe his own avowals—during the early days of this relationship. And would it not be this degree of love for which Erec was reproached by his friends during his overlong honeymoon with Enide? Such love, so violent as to make a man sick and lead a knight to lose all courage for battle, must necessarily be restrained and kept within a certain "measure." But Richard of Saint-Victor says nothing of this restraint. It serves his purpose simply to have pointed out the vehemence of conjugal love.

Love becomes even more intense in the following degrees, and it culminates in ecstasy. This is lawful rapture because it is related to God and not to a human being. However, even in connection with the fourth degree of love, in lines which betray his penetrating psychological insight that was based, according to his own witness, on personal observation, Richard writes:

In this state, love often turns into a kind of madness unless its impetus is restrained by great prudence and an equally great steadiness. There are often outbursts of temper between lovers in this state: they work up quarrels, and when there are no causes for enmity they seek false and often quite unlikely ones. In this state, love often turns into hatred since nothing can satisfy the lovers' mutual desire. Hence arises what we have often seen in some people, namely, that the more ardently they seem to love one another at first, the more they persecute each other afterwards with passionate hatred. Indeed, and this is even more astounding, at one and the same time they hate and yet do not cease to burn with desire for each other, and love in such a way that they do not desist from persecuting each other by hatred. Loving thus they hate, and hating they love, and strange to tell, hatred grows miserably by desire and desire by hatred. They endure fire and hail at the same time, since neither the heat of desire can dissolve the ice of hatred, nor can the hail of dislike extinguish the fire of passionate desire. Beyond measure, indeed contrary to nature, this fire burns more fiercely in water, for the conflagration of love flares up more strongly by the mutual conflict of opposites than it could by mutual peace.[15]

In this text Richard suggests that the sentiment of love can be ambiguous. Unless a man acts prudently, strong love can easily turn into hate. There is a paradox here and, as it were, a sort of vicious circle: love fosters hate, and hate fosters love. This happens when love, in itself an ambivalent whole, splits up into its negative and its positive elements. And it is precisely because these have not been welded together, integrated, that frustration sets in. In any true love relationship both the negative and the positive sentiments must be taken into account. Richard seems to have been aware of this and realized the existence of eventual conflictual dynamics in lovemaking.

This treatise has been recognized as being "Perhaps the most astonishingly animated mystico-speculative work in the mid-twelfth century."[16] This is true, but it is not unique in its kind. It is similar in many ways to Saint Bernard's description of the experience of love. This may be because Richard had read some of Bernard's texts, or else because they both had recourse to the themes offered by the Song of Songs, or again because they both drew upon universal symbols. Richard's style is less dense than Bernard's and more diffused. The abbot of Clairvaux insists more on the theological transpositions and Richard on the moral interpretation of a phenomenological experience. But when the latter expresses his conception of conjugal love—which is the subject under discussion here—it is evident that he had no experience of it. True, he admits marital love as being a positive value. But why, we may ask, does he confine it to the first degree of love? Why is the loving rapture in which the other degrees culminate, and which they describe progressively, excluded from human love and reserved to love for God?

Were the treatise on the four degrees of passionate love to have been written by a married man who was both a Christian and a theologian, it would certainly have been of a different nature. Richard had a certain experience of relations with God and it is this religious experience which he applies and tries to introduce when he describes marital relations of which he had no experience. He succeeds only partially because the union with God which he experienced in his monastery cannot be applied simply and purely to the relations existing between married people. The paradigm of marital relations must come from lived experience and not be fashioned after another and different experience foreign to marriage. It would be beyond the limits of the present study to make a deeper critical judgment of Richard's treatise. It is sufficient for our purpose here to point out to what extent he, too, in common with other authors, considers deep marital affection to be inherent to the condition of married partners.

Other Witnesses throughout the Century

Throughout the twelfth century there were other cloistral witnesses to the dignity of marriage. They sometimes wrote more briefly and consequently with less psychological nuances than those authors we have already studied. But, even at the risk of a certain monotony, it seemed necessary to bring them forward since they are revelatory of the attitude of a few among the many cloistral writers who held in esteem a state of Christian living which was beyond the pale of their own experience. Possibly this lack of marital experience helped them to speak more freely about marriage and with a certain optimism, as it is the tendency of men and women who are happy in the celibate life they have chosen to live to project their own peace and joy onto states of life other than their own.

A woman witness worthy of serious study is Saint Hildegard of Bingen, who wrote towards the middle of the century. There now exists a critical edition of her major work, the *Scivias,* and her *Hymnary.* But her other works, including those on physiology, should be examined too. With innocent realism she describes the normal activity of love, which she contrasts with the abnormal forms. She does not tolerate the "bestial impulsiveness of certain men." In that, as in everything else, Hildegard is a true woman. Unless it be that when she quotes God as saying, "You men. . . ." she has in mind the human race as a whole, men and women. Whatever may be, union in one flesh must always be a manifestation of union in charity.[17] Nothing should divide or disunite a married couple: they must both look in the same direction, toward the Son of God. Hildegard is one of those Christians who cannot imagine love without charity. If charity exists between married people, there is necessarily love, and if there is love, then it is the specific way of showing charity to each other. These two forms of freely chosen love are interdependent and reciprocally requisite. Charity without love, or love without charity—in adultery or fornication—are often real-life situations, but they are never the normal ones. The normal state is love in marriage accompanied with charity. Secular literature takes much delight in describing the abnormal situations in order to be more interesting and rouse the curiosity of their readers by narrating new adventures. But this in no way changes the Christian conception of conjugal love as being a form of charity. Monks and nuns who write about this conception of love repeat this incessantly and thereby risk idealizing reality. They sometimes do so with an artlessness which betrays their lack of experience. But such optimism, based on faith, is all to their honor. Hildebert of Mans is not a monk, but he writes to an abbess certain lines which are a continuation of the hymn to virgins in the Book of Revelation: "This Lamb, which the virgins follow, is followed too by those who dwell in widowhood and also by those who live in conjugality."[18]

It would be possible to find other witnesses of this monastic mentality who, throughout the century, wrote in lyrical terms on conjugal love. Not all were as prolix as those we have mentioned here. Some lay less stress on the inner dispositions of affection and bring out more the moralizing traditional prescriptions about the "measure" with which conjugal love should be used. Alan of Lille, for example, is more of the moralizing kind. However, in a sermon to married people, we find him exclaiming, "Oh! how great is the dignity of marriage!"[19] Adam of Perseigne, in a letter to the countess of Perche, "twice-married" to her husband and to her heavenly Lord, writes: "He is righteous, even more he is Righteousness itself. He instituted the law of marriage, and while you pay each one his rights, you practice heavenly righteousness."[20] Thus all the facts mentioned by the sententiaries at the beginning of the century concerning indulgence are harmonized with the fact that it is possible for married people to ally union in the flesh and union of heart and mind.[21]

A perfect example of such an optimistic approach is offered in the daily pastoral teaching of a man like Saint Hugh the Carthusian, who was bishop of Lincoln from 1186 until his death in 1200. He was chaste enough to have a guileless attitude toward women, and so was through them related to the Feminine. As did other bishops, he occasionally invited "devoted matrons" to eat at his table: "He used to lay his holy hands on their heads and make the sign of the cross and even sometimes reverently embrace them." And in words borrowed from the Song of Songs his biographer adds:

> . . . his words were to the hearts of those who heard them like wine sweet and fiery, and coming from one whom the King had taken into his wine cellar. . . . To lay persons who praised his angelic way of life and lamented the hindrances of life in the world, and whom he knew had neither the intention nor the capacity to follow a better way of life, he gave the following advice: "The kingdom of God is not confined only to monks, hermits and anchorites. . . all sincere Christians must have loving hearts, truthful tongues, and chaste bodies." The man of God often developed this further by describing and defending the properties and differences of these virtues. He taught that married people as well, who did not rise above the measure and limits of their state, should not be considered to be devoid of the virtue of chastity but equally with the virgins and celibates would be admitted to the glory of the heavenly kingdom.[22]

Besides the optimistic writers, there were probably, too, those who had a more severe approach, a more negative and pessimistic view of marriage. In general this seems to have been the case for minor authors with narrower minds and particularly when they wrote to clerics or religious to persuade them to remain faithful to the celibacy they had once freely chosen.

One of these pessimistic writers, a monk, having listed all the difficulties inherent to the married state, goes on to ask: "Does this mean that we consider the bonds of the marriage bed to be bad? Not at all." But, he goes on to add, they are not for religious.[23] Hugh of Fouilloy, recommending philosophers to "embrace spiritual espousals," advises them to abstain from those of the flesh.[24] We could also apply to religious tempted to be unfaithful to their celibacy this sally related toward the close of the twelfth century in a commentary on the Song of Songs attributed to Helinand of Froidmont: "The lustful say 'You theologians are very hard.' But Saint Jerome says 'The greatest show of kindness in this matter is to be cruel.' "[25]

It is interesting to speculate whether these texts penned by spiritual writers are any more representative of the general opinion on marriage than those of the sententiaries and the canonists, an opinion that was prevalent among Christians as a whole, nobles, burghers, villeins. And whether such writings influenced popular opinion. Whatever may be, it is certain that, throughout the twelfth century, canons and monks spread abroad by their writings a positive and healthy attitude toward marriage. Experts in law and the theology of marriage stated the principles in shorter and more dense texts, but their style was usually terse and abstract. Monastic authors explicated these principles in tones which were at once more poetic and more realistic. Thus, the sentences of a master in pastoral matters and the glosses of canonists were mainly restricted to the narrow circle of other and similar specialists, whereas the longer, more beautiful, and more accessible texts of the spiritual authors were more widely diffused. There is even a certain amount of discussion as to who was the best-seller of the twelfth century in matters of love, Hugh of Saint-Victor or Bernard of Clairvaux.[26] In fact it matters very little that statistics concerning the manuscript tradition of their works should attribute the laurels to either the one or the other. The truth remains that both were widely read and consequently had an influence, if only on preachers who, in their turn, published the ideas put forward by these two great authors.

A common factor in all writings or images concerning love is their aesthetic nature: there is beauty everywhere, and it does not seem that there is a specifically monastic theology on marriage as there is in other fields. Matrimonial problems were not the first concerns of monks, as they are quite naturally for others who are directly and permanently engaged in the pastoral care of married people. But in those few texts which have come down to us, we notice that cloistral writers expound the common teaching of the Church on matrimonial matters with greater beauty and poetry, in writings of a more highly developed literary genre, than we find in the statements of the sententiaries and the canonists who content themselves with the technical terms used in the schools.

A Cardinal, Singer of Nuptial Love

There is one last witness who ought to be associated with this literary and doctrinal trend: Cardinal Lotharius of Segni.[27] Before he became Pope Innocent III in 1198 he wrote a treatise on *The Four Weddings*.[28] He received his first literary and religious training at the monastery of Saint Andrew on the Caelion at Rome. When he became a canon of Saint Peter's, unlike many other clerics raised to ecclesiastical dignity, he continued to be faithful to the common life and liturgical prayer. A priest named Benedict, who was perhaps even a cardinal, asked him to write "a treatise on the wedding of the bride and bridegroom and to show the likenesses that exist between spiritual marriage and physical marriage, explaining in particular Psalm 44 that sings with such abundant praise the wedding of the bride and the bridegroom."[28] Benedict affirmed that he was not able to grasp the meaning of this biblical nuptial song. What seems to have been at stake was not the theology and the law relative to marriage—these were henceforth firmly established—but the religious sense of human marriage and how it could serve as a metaphor for other realities as Christian tradition held in connection with this psalm. It must be remembered that the errors put forth by the Cathars—by whatever name they went—were still being spread abroad during these times, and also that at the close of the twelfth century the growth of mendicant orders and the founding of universities, the first signs of the coming great social mutation which culminated in urbanization, was already beginning.

From the outset of his treatise, Lotharius adopts the traditional method which consisted in attributing to Holy Scripture four different senses rising from the realities expressed by the letter of the text to the increasingly elevated religious significations. In the case of matrimonial allegory these significations are related to the union of Christ and his Church, the union between God and a soul and that between the divine Word and human nature. But the basic fact is "fleshly union" in its "lawful" form, which is union between married people. Before commenting the psalm, Lotharius writes a long allegory in which all the elements of a wedding ceremony are first described and then applied to divine mysteries. The marriage ritual was greatly developed in those days and had been so for quite some time, even long before the twelfth century, at which point the presence of a priest was required for a marriage to be validly contracted.[29] Elements of folklore had been added to rites handed down from the ancient Roman tradition. Lotharius omits none of these details: the engagement, the promise of marriage, the dowry, the wedding gift, the bridesmaids, the witnesses, the incantation against evil, the ring, the passing of the ring over the finger, the bathing and anointing of the bride, the wedding garment, the crown, the praises of the bride's beauty, the kiss, the words of consent. Then the husband leads his newly wedded wife to his home and there, alone, in the intimacy which is proper to them, they unite. The last pages describe the banquet, the menu, the guests, the waiters. And throughout, from beginning to end, there is a constant transposition from the human to the divine level. The human is harmoniously allied to the divine while remaining a fact of real life, as in a wedding such as that described, for example, in *Erec and Enide*. The human is confronted and put into relation with the divine and the divine is expressed in the human, taking it as it is and giving it a richer and fuller meaning. All that happens on the physical, the psychological, and the psychosociological level is thus sublimated. In this perspective, celibacy is not seen as rejection of marriage but as an alternative leading to the full maturity of the biological, psychological, and spiritual being. And marriage becomes a means also of sharing in the love of God in Christ: God saves us in espousing us and helps us to understand his love for us through our own human love. United to God, man and woman, in celibacy or in marriage can deploy all their affective energies.

In this theological play there is, of course, something poetic, as in the romances. However, in both the one and the other it is real, existential, lived marriage which is the basic theme. In the text of Lotharius we find a few traditional formulas smacking of dualism and which possibly today certain people would prefer to ignore, such as the statement that "the body is to be loved less than the soul because it is in itself less than the soul."[30] But in this text, on the whole, every manifestation of a man's personal and social life is pressed into service for the highest form of love: that love which exists in God himself, love which was manifested and communicated to men in Christ and which is lived in the Church.

Only after this long and beautiful prelude does Lotharius embark upon his commentary of Psalm 44. This nuptial song is sung during the banquet to entertain the guests with musical accompaniment. The singer knocks at the door, but the porter, the *janitor,* before letting him into the banqueting hall asks him to prove that he is not one of those "jongleurs" or histrions who incite to adultery and other follies. A keen altercation goes on between them, and the king himself finally puts an end to the dispute, allowing the citharist to enter, who immediately starts singing the praises of the king and of the bridegroom. Here again, in connection with the psalm imagery, we can guess the whole contemporary social context: the Catharist errors about marriage; the battle of the Christians in the Holy Land; the influence of courtly literature; the reform of morals. We also see something of the handsome beauty of the bridegroom, his might and wisdom, his decorations and his sword. The biblical images are restrained and sober but mingled with images of medieval society: the portrait of the knight as well as of the just and honest judge. Lotharius renovates ancient themes by interpreting them in the light of contemporary culture, thus giving them renewed symbolic value. By updating ancient themes, he makes them even more eloquent, better suited to touch the hearts of his readers and lead them to mend their ways. He shows himself to be a poet, one of God's "jongleurs," as it were, in the same vein as Francis of Assisi, whom he was soon to applaud. In spite of this poetic strain in his treatise, Lotharius was also strong on principles and took doctrinal stands as Pope Innocent, especially on matters concerning marriage. He is then seen to be a quite rigid defender of the principles of law.[31]

FOUR

Ideals and Models

✤

The Relevance of Hagiography

The different ideas concerning the approach to marriage which we have so far gleaned from doctrinal texts are also to be found in another sort of literature: hagiography. Every society provides the models suiting its needs. In hagiographic literature we read of the marvelous deeds and the stirring examples—be they historical or or legendary—of heroes and saints. These are held up as being exceptional successes and, literally, extraordinary in the living out of a life project proposed to every man and woman. And, as for every other literary genre, historiography always contains a certain dose of exaggeration which must be taken into consideration. In this particular case, the exaggeration appears under the form of idealization. However, though the authors do not intend to propose models which we can imitate, nevertheless they endeavor to situate their heroes in historical circumstances and a cultural context which helps us to grasp that they lived in our own real world and not in some idealized world. Consequently, we should make some effort to follow in their footsteps. Furthermore, in contrast to secular texts which were soon forgotten and lay hidden under the dust of ages until discovered and edited by present-day scholars who sometimes have to work on a restricted number of manuscripts, the hagiographical narrations, in successive redactions, were read, generation after generation, at least in the place where or for which they had been composed. And, often enough, they were read in other places too. Generally, such stories were meant to be read aloud and listened to during divine office. Thus it is that certain texts, written at an earlier date, witness to a mentality which had survived and was still prevalent in the twelfth century. The particular interest of hagiography is that it enables us to study the evolution of thought and practice by tracing down the constant emphasis laid by the collective memory on certain models. In the Middle Ages, the major cultural and religious influence molding this collective conscience was Christianity. This does not infer, however, that the medieval mind-set did not also reflect the universal archetypal symbols and models studied by depth psychology and ethnology. In the Christian tradition, as in all others, these texts "live on," so to speak: they are amplified and modified by fresh interpretations made possible by new sociocultural facts. For this reason they can be used as witnesses only if they are replaced in the past historical context in which they were originally set.

In the twelfth century, all the knowledge accumulated by theological, canonical, and spiritual thinking is projected, as it were, onto biographies and portraits of holy men and women, offering a pretext for showing how these ideas fitted into the life of certain Christians. In the field of the attitude to marriage, all possible cases come up. The major convictions stated in the Lives may be summed up in the following points: there is no marriage without freedom of choice; conjugal love does not necessarily imply consummation; union in the flesh is one of the means by which married people can sanctify both self and one's partner. An exhaustive inquiry would reveal witnesses to these different cases and show to what extent each one is dealt with in the texts. But once again, all we can do here is to quote a few of the more important examples.

Freedom to Choose as a Condition for Marriage

The first fact which twelfth-century theory and practice made clear was that there is no lawful marriage without previous freedom of choice. Such freedom concerns the choice to marry or not to marry and, in the case of the wish to marry, to choose one's partner. It had been one of the first ways of asserting Christian freedom before the eyes of the world, especially for women, to assert the right to refuse marriage and all the violence which was sometimes implied in ancient civilizations and in those which developed from the barbarian invasions. And, let it be said in passing, such a state of coercion and violence still exists in many clan societies of the non-Western world today. It is probably this preference given to celibacy over marriage which is the most amply illustrated in hagiography.

Examples are found throughout the twelfth century, and they are often narrated in picturesque and exciting stories similar to those of the romance literature. One such story is that of Oda of Bonne Espérance.[1] She was a nun of the Premonstratensian Order who died in 1159. Philip of Harvengt wrote her *Life*. As in other noble families, her parents decided upon her marriage and chose a partner for her. However, enough freedom was left her so that finally it was she who decided, as provided for by the ritual. Oda, while still young, had decided to become a nun in the convent of Bonne Espérance, which was quite near the family manor. Philip tells the story of her life, sprinkling his account with reminiscences from the two biblical wedding songs, Psalm 44 and the Song of Songs. The whole account could be divided up into "acts" and "scenes," as were the ancient tragedies and those written by Hrotswitha.

Oda confided her secret to a young cousin and asked him to go and tell it to the abbot of Bonne Espérance. But the young cousin proved to be an unfaithful friend and betrayed her secret to her parents. They called together a great family gathering and decided to find a suitor for her. This they did in the person of a certain Simon, who agreed to marry Oda. The two families came to an agreement and the date of the marriage was fixed. In a long soliloquy, Oda gives vent to her sorrow and distress, ratifying before God her decision. Before the marriage, the news is spread abroad, the house is decorated with carpets, and the whole family puts on new and festive garb. They busy themselves about the wedding dress and accessories of the bride-to-be, who nevertheless remains sad. Her father, noticing his daughter's melancholy, holds forth in a soliloquy and then tries to persuade her to enjoy her youthful days and her fortune. He even lies and says that he is willing to put off the marriage till a later date if that would please her, and she, innocently, thinks that she has won the day.

The next morning, a whole crowd of relatives and friends in full dress gathers in the court (*curia*) of the castle because the church is too far away. The bride and bridegroom come in. Oda enters with the determination of one going to fight in the arena. "According to custom, the priest asks Simon three times in succession if he willingly consents lawfully to marry Oda." After the answer in the affirmative, the same question is put to the bride, who bows her head and says nothing. The question is asked a second time, but Oda still remains silent. A lady who is a close friend of the family tries to persuade her to answer and to consent. But Oda refuses to answer the second and even the third time that the question is put to her. Everyone urges her to speak. She does so only to express her refusal to marry. Surprise and confusion among all present. Simon declares he is offended and will not marry a dumb woman. He gets on his horse and goes back home. Oda's parents, disgraced, severely rebuke her, and her father angrily declares before everyone that he will oblige his daughter to marry whether she will or not. She, profiting by the general commotion, escapes secretly and runs back home. There she locks herself into her mother's room and begs God to help her. "Seizing a sword hanging over the bed (a detail which tells us much about the violence of those times) she tries to cut off her nose. But her hand trembles: she is not used to wielding such a weapon and the bony part of her nose resists." She harangues the sword which has refused to mutilate her beauty, then, "outdoing her strength," she manages to cut the side of her nose, and blood flows abundantly from the wound into a basin. The family arrives, starts looking for her, and, hearing her talking to herself and praying aloud, they knock at the door, summoning her to open. Finally, they break down the door with hatchet and hammer and find her disfigured, almost bloodless. Her mother entreats her; her father arrives on horseback; everyone is weeping except Oda. She appeals to the abbot of Bonne Espérance, who arrives with two of his religious. The father feigns receiving them graciously but hastens to add that he will not allow his daughter to have her way. Among the reasons he invokes are the family fortune and the material advantages to be gained by the marriage. Oda claims the right to freedom and threatens her father that she will disobey him later if he forces her to marry. Finally, he gives in to her, the abbot of Bonne Espérance approves, and she bids farewell to her family. The account of the sequence of events and the accompanying spiritual considerations are worthy of the theologian who was Philip of Harvengt. When Oda dies, the Song of Songs is quoted one last time to evoke the transition from her espousals with her heavenly bridegroom in this present life to their full realization in the life after death. But the major and unifying idea throughout the whole story is the theme of freedom to marry or not to marry.

We have another text, the *Life of Christine of Markyate*, which illustrates the vicissitudes of this question of free choice in matters of marriage and celibacy. The question is related to a legal procedure which shows that for want of consent it could be queried whether or not a marriage had been contracted or whether it was to be declared nul. Christine ended up as a recluse near the Abbey of Saint Albans. Through the intermediary the abbot Geoffrey, she is said to have influenced not only the monastery, but even the whole kingdom.[2] In her *Life,* written at Saint Albans between 1145 and 1155, we read that many times she refused to accept marriage whether the pressure came from her family or from the clergy. She even had occasion to refuse fornication. In fact, her *Life* is a sort of *Historia calamitatum* recounting in reverse all that happened to Abelard and Héloïse. It is a true adventure novel, describing as many trials and tribulations as we find in the romances of courtly literature. The various trials and tests which Christine has to undergo give her ample opportunity of proving that she does not refuse marriage out of contempt but because she is in love with another Bridegroom, Christ. Such is indeed the major theme of this romance of freely chosen celibacy.

Happy Marriages without Consummation

Besides the freedom to choose, there is another conviction which emerges from twelfth-century doctrinal writings on marriage, namely, the necessity of love. The marriage act is considered to be a normal but not indispensable manifestation of such love. Two logical consequences of this second conviction are that conjugal love is in no way lessened by nonconsummation and that carnal union outside marriage is a sin against such love. These truths are illustrated by narratives describing human behavior and confirming the ideas expressed in more speculative terms by theologians, canonists, and anti-catharist polemists.

First of all there is a series of writings which can be used as evidence in favor of marriage without consummation but not without love. It is even sometimes explicitly stated that in such cases love is not only present but that it is even more intense because spiritual. Legends of this kind develop a traditional theme in hagiography from the first centuries of the Church up to our own times.[3] Figments of the imagination? Maybe! But if we find any significance in the Arthurian or other legends, what right have we to refuse to delve into legends about marriage with the purpose of discovering the conception of love they imply or propose? For, even if the Lives cannot be considered as historical evidence, their teaching remains more important than any events, be they real or imagined. Such events as are narrated were only pretexts allowing the authors to expose their doctrines. Such narratives are sometimes real romances of virginal love. The adventures they relate are no less thrilling than those invented by the authors of secular romances. Thus, the *Life of Saint Amalberg,* written in the tenth century and subsequently read by generations of clerics and nuns in choir, brings before our eyes the trials through which this virgin comes unscathed; through love, she remains faithful to Christ her spouse even though his rival is no less a personage than the emperor Charlemagne, who, "carried away by love for her, would not desist from asking her hand in marriage through the solicitations of intermediaries."[4] It is worth noting that the reason he gave for wanting to marry her was that he loved her.

In the same way, the historical fact of the unfruitful marriage between the emperor Henry II (d. 1024) and Saint Cunegund was soon transformed into a story which was later to give rise to other edifying romances[5] and iconographical themes, such as the testing by fire to which Cunegund was submitted, as is related by a Bamberg manuscript of the twelfth century.[6] It is for the historians to decide, if they can, whether the unfruitfulness was the result of sterility or of impotence,[7] but the fact remains that an addition to the Life at the beginning of the thirteenth century makes it out to be a romance of virginal, reciprocal love. So this is something which existed at least in the mind of the author and his readers. But the story also illustrates clearly that genuine marital effection does not require genital expression. The married partners came to be so intimate with each other that the empress became the adviser of her husband in affairs of state, an unusual eventuality. All through the story the writer stresses this "affection" and love.[8] Though it was an arranged marriage, it was also accepted fully, or, as we would say today, it was an "integral" marriage. Cicero's definition of friendship is applied to the partners: "They both desired the same things or alternatively did not want them, even to the point where if one of them undertook to do something, the other would take steps to dispatch it. . . ." They "loved each other tenderly" with "a spiritual love."[9] When enemies took advantage of a journey that the emperor had to make alone and calumniated his wife, he ended up by believing in her infidelity and "his heart quivered within him and he was profoundly sad. He decided to see her no more." The slandered empress for her part "was exceedingly distressed, wounded by love, she desired to see her beloved again with an ardent longing. One day she seized an opportunity to approach him, and burning with love and tender feelings, she greeted him with all possible affection."[10] We cannot go into all the adventures, but they end up happily and lead to reconciliation. The scholarly editor of the text classifies it in his short introduction as being "full of fables,"[11] but why should this long fabliau seem less illuminating than others which deal with the love-story theme? In the mind of the author and of his readers a marriage which was arranged for political reasons could perfectly well become a love match.

There are two early texts which deserve special attention for two reasons: first because they show that ancient themes were still in vigor in the Middle Ages, including the twelfth century, and secondly, because they either witness strongly to conjugal love or illustrate it in literary style. The first of these texts is the *History of Appolonius, King of Tyre*. It is a mysterious text. The Latin version seems to date from the sixth century and certainly contains some Christian elements. It was used throughout the Middle Ages and was translated into several languages, including English in the eleventh century. Several writers, including a monk of Saint-Omer, Lambert, gave many romanced developments of it, and its influence has been detected even in Shakespeare. It contains one sentence in particular which is of such conciseness in Latin that it almost defies translation: *Iugis amor fit inter coniuges, mirus affectus, incomparabilis dilectio, inaudita laetitia, quae perpetua caritate complectitur.*[12] It would be difficult to use in fewer lines so many words expressing affection, consent, the joy of love and charity. And we know for sure that this kind of literature was as prolific as were the legends of King Arthur or Tristan.

Another witness of this literature which so constantly reflects the psychology and the spirituality of the milieux where they were rewritten is the series of redactions of the legend of Saint Alexius. He consented to marriage but from the very first night refused to consummate it and persuaded his wife to accept this continence. The text, of early origin, was translated into Latin toward the end of the tenth century. The author of the *Life of Christine of Markyate* had knowledge of this text and the *Life,* in its turn, influenced the development of the legend: it would seem that the French text of the *Cançun de Saint Alexis* is inspired by Christine's adventures.[13] According to the original story of the Life of Alexius, he obtained in a single night what she had to fight for during years of struggle. When Alexius accepted his parents' proposition about marriage, he gave his reason saying, "Because of the divine precept, I know that marriage will not be a sin for me, but a grace; so I will do what you ask." Afterwards he told his wife that he intended to separate from her without having consummated their union, and she accepted without resistance.[14] In the *Cançun* this is related at length and seasoned with adventure stories. The way this romanced narration tells of the relations between man and wife on their wedding night and all through life up to the death of Alexius, and even beyond, gives us an insight into the well-defined juridical and social problems in cause. From the literary and psychological point of view, it is interesting to note that in France, at the time of the first courtly romances, it happened that the same writer wrote for the same public two different styles of work: religious or profane adventure and love stories, with or without the marriages being consummated.

Likewise, when the legend of Mary the Egyptian—a converted harlot who became a recluse—is rewritten in French, it becomes a true romance very like those of courtly literature. The new drafts added to the primitive lives troubled and hardly credible episodes, exciting details, all presented with intentions very different from those of profane romances. In these the aim was to provide amusement. In the French Life, though this is not excluded, it becomes edifying. In both instances, the underlying ethics presupposed and illustrated are not at all the same. But the literary expression often remains similar, for example in the description of womanly beauty or the wiles by which Mary enticed her clients before her conversion.[15] In the evolution of the legend, the boundaries between hagiography and romance are no longer clearly defined. But in the romance which developed out of the legend, charity, even when clothed in the language of courtly love, continues to be a specifically Christian attitude. During her life as a solitary, Mary had a trusted and confidential friend with whom she has a deep spiritual friendship. But both live and die in a state of love from afar, an *amor de longh*.

At the end of the thirteenth century, another Cunegund, Queen of

Poland, "haggled," so to speak, with the man she was to marry, Boleslas by name, and she first of all obtained from him one year of virginity, for his love of her, then a year for the love of the Mother of God.[16] Meanwhile her confessor, arguing from Holy Writ, showed her that she ought to agree to union with the king. But even though battered with arguments from the Old and the New Testaments, Church history, and Church law, she still hesitated and then, refuting all the reasons, gave the learned priest a severe dressing-down and at last ran away and refused to listen any more. Nevertheless, the succession to the throne was in question, so the king's advisers took him to task for all the concessions he had made to his wife. Widespread political agitation swept through Poland, as there was fear that the kingdom would be divided in the event of failure to secure an heir. The king left her and never wished to see her again. Up to this point in the story of this arranged marriage and virginal love, there does not seem to have been any love between the two, but through the prayers of Saint John the Baptist, the king changed his mind and even came round to making a downright declaration of chaste love. Cunegund herself was a real helper to the king in political matters, "she prayed for her earthly husband" and for the success of his battles, and she remained faithful to her heavenly spouse. All Poland was grateful to her. She made the king accept the fact that the succession should pass to another hereditary line, and she even persuaded him to make a vow of continence and to separate from her so that she could become a Franciscan tertiary, and to agree that when he died she should become a nun.[17] Besides all this she managed to affect the reconciliation of an unhappily married couple, after she had converted the adulterous husband;[18] she knew that marriage required love and fidelity. It is enough to convince us that neither in her mind nor in the mind of her hagiographer—nor in anyone else's—are these unconsummated marriages to be presented as models for the imitation of Christians in general. They are to be seen as extreme cases, all pointing to the fact that marriage, whether consummated or not, is based on love.

Shortly after the beginning of the thirteenth century, Jacques de Vitry reminds us of this fact in the *Life* he wrote of Mary d'Oignies, who died in 1213. He even goes so far as to state clearly that not all things done by the saints are necessarily to be imitated.[19] This is true of the relations between Mary and her husband John after he had offered to help her live in continence. But, says Jacques in words that might seem paradoxical, from that time on their love became even more ardent: "The more he lived apart from her according to love in the flesh, the more closely was he bound spiritually to her by the bonds of freely chosen love (*dilectio*)."[20]

Conjugal Love with Consummation

Examples of holy men and women who consummated marriage are also found in medieval hagiography. There are probably more accounts of holiness in and by the celibate state.[21] But they should not lead us to forget that there exist other holy people who lived in consummated, fruitful, and happy love. Some of these people lived in this state of love in consummation until their death. Others renounced it, by common consent with their partner, in order to become monks or nuns. For others, again, widowhood ended happy married love. This last case should be placed in the general context of what we know on the evolution in the Church of the "power to dissolve" and its use in the twelfth century. For each of the three categories mentioned, it would be possible to draw up a list of documents. But for our present purpose the important thing is to pick out the explicit or implicit witnesses to conjugal love. The point to be illustrated is that God must have the first place, in whatever state of life, and that partners must render to God what is God's and to each other what is due. This is a conception which is even found in a tenth-century text, the *Life of Saint Ida of Herfeld,* illustrating the fact with a poetic elegance and a realistic precision of detail which herald the way in which Saint Bernard was to make a theological application of the conjugal metaphor. This text contains an extremely dense phrase which says that it is in the very marriage act itself that Ida and her husband, Count Egbert, are united in a single act and operation of the Holy Spirit (*duobus in carne una unam inesse Spiritus Sancti indivisam operationem*). The rest of the narration illustrates this union of two loves in one. The theological statement is contained in a long account of which we can only give a summary here. The text was composed by Uffing, a monk of Werden, and it was read at divine office in the monasteries of the region.[22] According to the author, Ida, a daughter of a noble family, helped to nurse Count Egbert, who had fallen sick. He falls in love with her and the families propose that they marry. And this they do, knowing that after their death they will share the same reward in heaven. They were truly "companions of eternity." Ida persuades Egbert to build a church at Herzfeld. They have several children, five of whom survive, and their destinies are typical of what generally happened in those days: one of their sons became an abbot, one of the daughters became an abbess, another was a nun in the abbey to which the mother retired; the two other sons married noble ladies and held high office in society. Ida was successful in conciliating the two loves of which her biographer writes: "Though she was bound by the law of marriage, she preferred nothing to the love of her heavenly bridegroom." All that she did, in fact, was simply to observe the commandment binding on all Christians and by which we are to love God above all. "Because of that," says Uffing, "she in no way suffered damage to the modesty of her chastity." Chastity here means fidelity to the heavenly bridegroom. "Even more, she was rewarded a hundredfold, as were in the Gospel (Mt. 20) the works of the last hour." It is worth pointing out that the number one hundred was the symbol of the reward offered to virgins. "She received it because she was victorious over vice."

How did she do this? First, she prayed much, thus showing that her love for God was foremost. In a dense Latin phrase which it is scarcely possible to translate in all its force, Uffing, writing of Ida's marital relations with her husband, explains that during intercourse she was careful to render to God what was his due, so measuring her love according to the flesh that her mind was in no way sullied by unbecoming frivolousness. In this way she safeguarded the rights of both her heavenly and her earthly spouse and observed the Christian principle which requires that everything be done with fitting measure. And Uffing goes on to say, "Indeed, if it is true, as Saint Paul teaches (1 Cor. 7: 14), that the unbelieving husband is sanctified through his believing wife, then how much more true is it that both partners become vessels of holiness when they differ in virtue." For expressing the truth of this fact of two virtues in a single holiness, there is nothing more appropriate than the Pauline metaphor which applies to union with God what the Book of Genesis (2: 24) and the Gospel of Saint Matthew (19: 5–6) say of marital union. Uffing states this in the daring words which have already been quoted in Latin above: "At the time of their being two in one flesh, there is within them a one and only operation of the Holy Spirit: at the time of their embrace in the bonds of outer, tangible love, this invisible working of the Holy Spirit fires them to a greater inner love for heavenly realities." Deep human love between man and wife is accompanied with even greater love of both the one and the other for God. The Bollandist who edited this phrase, in his embarrassment or perhaps his skepticism, added a comment to the effect that he left it to others to explain. And, effectively, an interpretation will be found in the writings of Saint Bernard, as we shall see.

Some years after his marriage with Ida, Egbert dies and she gives herself up entirely to a life of asceticism and contemplative prayer. She has a chapel built for herself next to the church built by her husband, on the very spot where he is buried, and it is there that she gives herself to a life of prayer in faithful communion with him. She only leaves her reclusion when she goes to look after the poor. "See then how she honors her widow's veil, how she endeavors to attain to perfect charity, how she loves her heavenly bridegroom, how she merits the reward reserved to virgins." In this context, virginity is confirmed by a spiritual rather than a physical state. When Ida dies she commits her spirit to her heavenly lover and is buried beside Egbert. Their bodies are united in the grave forever. Later, another Christian member of their family, revered as a model of chastity, is laid to rest with them. In this way, this long story is a witness to chastity from beginning to end, woven around the life of a holy woman who lived as a happy wife and mother and ended her days as a widow faithful to her husband's memory. In both states of life she constantly allied love for a man and love for Christ.

Still another twelfth-century witness is the Life of Saint Pauline, who died in 1107. The Life was composed around 1150 by Sigiboto, a monk of Hirsau. In the preface we read that "Christ loves the doctors (i.e., the priests), he loves married people, and he loves those who live in celibacy." It is then recalled how, during his preaching ministry, "married women and widows accompanied him with much devotion and ministered to their Lord, drawing on their own resources." After such introductory words, we are not surprised to learn that Pauline's parents, "united by matrimonial fidelity and conjugal society, rendered to Caesar what was Caesar's and to God what was God's." Her mother, then, though she was bound by the ties of marriage and faithful to the marriage bed, "did not forget the bridegroom of her soul." When she became a widow she remarried, under pressure from her family, though she would have preferred not to do so. However, "once she was associated to her new husband's bed, she gave herself entirely to him and did not deny him his conjugal rights." Sigiboto insists, in a manner which is slightly shocking for our modern mentalities, upon the feelings of the merry widow: she feels free now that her husband is dead, "even though she loved him greatly." But she is not sad. On the contrary, she is happy, for she has another bridegroom, Christ. "And she embraces the continence proper to widows with the same freedom of mind as that which had once allowed her to safeguard the rights of conjugal reserve."[23]

Hagiography is a world unto itself. We are all free to choose, in keeping with our tastes, or the particular thesis we wish to illustrate, the texts which best suit our purpose. Some of these texts leave no doubt as to the prevailing mind on marital affection in every age; for example, in the ninth century we find "the sensuousness of marital union" mentioned in the *Life of Harthumoda* written by Agius of Corbie. It figures among the different facts which, according to the use which is made of them, can be either good or bad, like any other of the pleasures of life.[24] At the beginning of the eleventh century, we find it written of Saint Mathilda and her husband, King Henry I of Germany, that they took pleasure in their marriage and in lawful loving union. She remained faithful to the commitments of marriage. "Sometimes at night, she rose stealthily from the marriage bed, as though the king were unaware, and went to pray." But it is hardly credible that she could do this without her husband knowing. He was aware enough of it, but he feigned ignorance, for he knew that all she did was for his good as well as her own. Subtle delicacy of marital love! And "God gave increase to their noble progeny."[25]

Towards the close of the eleventh century or the beginning of the twelfth, a Benedictine of Durham who wrote the *Life of Margaret, Queen of Scots* (d. 1093) uses in half a sentence the word *love* and the verb *to love* twice each for describing the dispositions which her husband Malcolm III showed in her favor: *Quae ipsa respuerat, eadem et ipse respuere, et quae amaverat, amore amoris illius amare.* . . . He sought every possible way of showing that he loved her. He could not read, but he handled and looked lovingly at her prayer books, kissing and gently stroking the one she said she liked best. He asked his goldsmith to bind it with a cover decorated with gold and precious stones. Margaret and Malcolm had six sons and two daughters.[26]

Another story is told in the *Life of Saint Bernard,* a monk of Schaffhausen who died in 1075. His mother Hedwige also rose to pray during the night, but this did not please her husband Eppo. One night, while she was asleep, he quietly got up from beside her, took her psalter, and threw it into the kitchen fire. However, the next day when the cook came to work, he found the book lying undamaged on the grill. Eppo learnt the lesson and henceforth shared his wife's devotions.[27]

Later on we read about the parents of Saint Geoffrey of Savigny. "Both of them, in marital religion, behaved with all honesty. For the service of God and their own relief they begot five sons, by the grace of divine bounty."[28] The Latin word *solatium* used here may be taken to correspond with the word *solaz* used in courtly literature.

Another example of a happily married couple is described by the chronicler William of Tyre and depicted in some of the Bayeux tapestries. William writes of Ida of Lorraine (1040–1113) that "she had the grace and the art of being loved by her husband" Eustace, count of Boulogne. "She knew the joys of a happy union," and it is said that she insisted on breast-feeding herself three of her sons. William of Tyre describes "this very gentle and very gay" mother playing with her children in the upper room of the castle where they are joined by the young and happy father, her husband. One last detail deserves notice: "The life of the castle went on in two main rooms. On the ground floor there was the Hall, a state room where the count received his guests, held audience and council meetings. His wife was one of his advisers at least for administrative and financial questions."[29]

These are but a few of the many examples which are waiting to be collated at the cost of exhaustive research. The same conciliation between love for God, marital love, and the duties of a wife and mother is suggested in the twelfth century, though more briefly in connection with the holiness of the mother of Saint Bernard and the mother of Peter the Venerable. They were both happy wives and gave birth to several children.[30] It is to be noted that the examples quoted here prove that an authentic human love is quite in keeping with exemplary Christian conduct.

FIVE

Witnesses to the
Common Reality
⚜

Daily Life: Exempla

J ust as in profane literature we find long romances, fabliaux, short poems, and short stories, so likewise in religious literature, besides the doctrinal treatises and the lives, we find many texts which have not always been given the attention they deserve: these are the exempla which were either written or taken out from longer documents and then put together in anthologies. They were intended for the use of preachers who wished to illustrate their sermons. There are literally thousands of them, many of which were already in circulation in the twelfth century. A great proportion concerned husbands, wives, and adulterous people. This is evident from the index of the repertory published by F. C. Tubach.[1] And it would even seem that some of the fabliaux grew out of an incident narrated in one or other of the exempla. Both kinds of text are dependent on the same culture and betray the same moralizing concern. Their didactic methods are often similar and based on the same models.[2] In the exempla the tone is more serious and less ironical, the style less realistic. They are quite often humorous. Spiritual writings analyze the inner and complex attitudes of religious souls striving after deep union with God, whereas the domestic scenes presented in the exempla depict the actions and spontaneous feelings of Christians engaged in ordinary, everyday life. And just as the writers of lives imagine situations which afford pretexts for stressing the importance of love, so other writers invent other and different situations in which the absence of love is shown to be evil. This whole field deserves careful research with a particular attention to the place given in the exempla to both matrimonial fidelity and to adultery, which is its opposite. These short texts are often picturesque: they reveal a very real society whose problems were the same as in every other age and place. For instance, in the field of married life, the main problems concern free consent, fidelity, the risk of infidelity, widowhood and remarriage, interventions of the mothers-in-law, temptations, adultery, the role of prostitution, the Christian attitude towards harlots, inspired by Christ's own attitude, and so on.

There is scarcely any idealization in this literature: evil and sin are considered and acknowledged as being infractions of morality. But this very human society is also Christian: prayer, grace, the sacraments, the ministry of the Church, the interventions of God and the saints make possible reconciliation of the people not only among themselves, but also with the Church and with God. They show that this society is not permissive but comprehensive. Evil is denounced for what it is, but there is room for comprehension, indulgence, forgiveness, and these attitudes are often expressed with humor and joy, with imagination and compassion, all so many proofs of an intense vitality.

The list of examples drawn up by Tubach contains almost fifty-six hundred stories. And this figure must be multiplied because many of the texts are repeated in different series, each one of which exists in several manuscript copies. Some of the exempla are later than the twelfth century and this must be taken into account. Even so, they are often dependent on sources redacted during the twelfth century or before it. The vast number of such texts shows what great importance such writings had in the collective memory. In these stories a certain place is given to the marvelous, but this in no way detracts from the realism of the situation described.

To limit our inquiry to the exempla which we are sure were written during the twelfth century and which are transmitted by monastic texts, we can begin by quoting some of those found in the *Miracula* of William of Malmesbury. He mentions celibacy and marriage, and this is a reminder that these two states had something in common: in both the one and the other, at least according to the Church's intention, it is supposed that men and women, having taken a free decision in their adult years, are greatly in love, either with God or with a fellow being, and even—why should it not be so?—with both.

Let us take the example of a cleric at Pisa who inherits a fortune.

His friends and his family do all they can to turn him away from his vocation. Giving way an instant to human frailty, he agrees to marry: he chooses a young girl who, though she is willing, is still too young. So he has to wait, and we can imagine the struggles he had with himself during this delay. When the wedding day finally comes, the Virgin Mary calls the cleric to repentance. So at midnight, when all the guests are falling asleep through overdrinking, he escapes.[3]

Another cleric is trusted by his bishop. But while the cleric is away at studies, he dabbles in the "forbidden arts," black magic. As a result of this, he forces every young woman whom he chooses to kiss him, even if he has to fight with her. According to the general tittle-tattle, any woman upon whom he cast his evil eye was seduced. Only one succeeded in resisting him, because she was given to chastity. So he calls the Devil to his aid. The Devil promises to help him if he will deny Christ and Our Lady. This he refuses, but he is willing to concede anything else. The Devil then influences the girl, who threatens to commit suicide if she is not allowed to come together with the cleric. Now, she is noble, but he is not. The bishop lets himself be persuaded that it is better for the cleric to marry than to fornicate, and he not only dispenses him from celibacy but gets the parents to consent to the marriage of their daughter. They are engaged and the wedding date is fixed. But during the nuptial Mass, the cleric is reciting the Hours of the Blessed Virgin. She appears to him, strikes up a conversation with him during which he tells of his true friendship for her. Thus she is able to convert him, and repenting, he weeps while the Virgin consoles him. He then hastens off to confess everything to his bishop, who dissolves the marriage and separates the couple as easily as he had approved of their union, "because he was a sincere and honest man." Such is the flexibility of the law! And the understanding of those who enforce it! The importance, too, of inner dispositions, freedom, and love! After this torment of his youthful days, our cleric lives a holy life until the end.[4]

Then there is the story about the jealous wife, narrated by William of Malmesbury[5] and other monks, Guibert of Nogent,[6] Gautier of Cluny.[7] William places the event at the time of Lambert, bishop of Arras from 1093 to 1115. Each narrator gives more or less details, and there are some differences as to the way in which the Virgin Mary intervened miraculously. But the interest of the tale lies in the circumstances of social life and the feelings expressed by the different people—and on this point there is unanimity. A husband, of whom Gautier says he is a man of the people, of the common crowd (*plebeiae multitudinis vir*), left his lawful wife and went to live with another woman. The wife is "distressed because the loving embrace of the adulteress was preferred to her own." She is in a constant state of fury and every day cries out for vengeance to the Mother of God, begging her to do her justice in the face of her rival. Her pleadings with the Virgin are presented by Guibert with precise legal terms: he speaks of an appeal in justice, the word clamor occurs several times in the text, Mary is addressed as Lady and Queen (*domina, regina*), and appeal is made to her justice (*iustitia*) and her power (*potestas*). Mary uses the same words in her answer. The fact is, however, that though the jealous wife is within her rights, her heart is full of hate. The harlot, on the contrary, is always gentle. Both women pray to Mary, but the way in which they do so reveals two very different attitudes. The first, the lawful wife "demands," whereas the other "hails" Mary with the words of the archangel Gabriel. This is more pleasing to Mary and she refuses to intervene against someone who gives her such pleasure. One day the two women meet each other and there is a violent scene. The deceived wife, furious, insults the other, follows her into the midst of the crowd, and tries to hit her. But the harlot answers nothing evil back, and the crowd is in her favor against the angry wife. Everything ends happily with a double miracle: the sinful woman (*peccatrix mulier*) confesses her sin and, according to Gautier, lives faithfully as a recluse until her death. As for the other woman, she recovers her husband and her peace of soul. She never accepted the adulterous situation. But one of the points of the story is to show that hatred is worse than shamelessness. Social pressure also has an influence in this direction. Finally, adultery is not only a transgression of matrimonial fidelity but also a source of intense suffering for the deceived wife, who says to the other woman: "What anguish you have caused my soul. You who by your caresses have taken away from me my very flesh!" This shows how the people considered the marriage ties.

The three examples which have just been outlined only sketch some of the problems connected with marriage, because, on the one hand, the stories were penned by monks, and on the other hand the point of the stories is to extol the Virgin Mary. Other accounts which are less "mystical" and more "pastoral" would possibly evoke other situations insisting less on celibacy and more on the duties of married couples. But at least the examples cited illustrate three complementary values of a loving life in the twelfth century: clerics should live in chastity; girls may vow their virginity to God; married people should be faithful to one another.

Towards the end of the century a monk of Clairvaux who had become abbot of Eberbach devoted long pages to a story in which he applies the method taught by one of his contemporaries who, as we have already seen, wrote a handbook for confessors in which wives are advised to do good to their husbands through love. Here is part of the story:

> There was once a soldier who was graced with nobility, riches, and the great manly strength of his youthfulness. And, puffed up by his fleshly appetites, he despised the laws of God and man. Defying civil and natural rights, he had little care as to whether fire, plundering, sedition, and murder were right or wrong, and to sum up shortly all his evil deeds we can say that "he neither feared God nor regarded man." But he had a faithful wife given up to the piety of the Christian religion, as much as was possible with such a cruel husband. She, loving her husband with sincere charity (*virum suum sincera caritate diligens*), wept unceasingly because of his wickedness and poured out her prayers to the Lord for his conversion, moved as she was by a spiritual rather than a carnal love. Especially when she saw that his violent spirit was even so slightly carried away by anger and that the joy and serenity of his countenance was overclouded, she began to approach him with gentle rebuke and besought him with many tears and much exhortation that he cease a little from such evil ways and placate the Lord by the humility of penance and confession. But he, now by a very dangerous deceitfulness, now by rowdy indignation, spurned his noble wife, she who was so anxious for his salvation, saying that he was not yet willing to repent, but that rather he intended to go on warring and fighting. He said he could not suffer the shame of his kinsmen and the reproach of his friends, if by laziness and want of energy he should fail to retaliate by an evil double or even triple that which his enemies did him. But even though she was often rebuffed in this way, his noble wife never broke down in despair. And when, moved by holy desire, she lent herself to her husband's embrace, she continued in season and out of season to proffer chaste advice, even though she was not asked to do so, until at last, overcome by her persistent kindness and

softened by his wife's charity (*uxoria quoque caritate delinitus*), he said to her, "Look, I want to follow your advice."

The rest of the story relates his difficulties with a confessor who tells him to go to the pope for absolution. This angers the would-be penitent and he goes back to his wicked ways and even cuts off the priest's head. Afterwards he tells his wife what he has done. She turns pale and almost faints away. However, she does not rebuke him harshly. But "the love which issues from a pure heart and a good conscience and sincere faith" which was deeply rooted in her breast overcame all difficulties and obstacles and she struck with the hammer of love which is strong as death to overcome evil. The more he pushed her away, the more she gently but firmly insisted and was victorious in the end, for, as the Apostle says, "the unbelieving husband is sanctified through his wife."

Other texts of the same genre are to be found at every period of the twelfth century. But we must close our short inquiry. A few examples given by a witness towards the end of the century will serve as a conclusion. In his unedited commentary on the Song of Songs, the Cistercian Helinand of Froidmont mentions a wicked woman who punched her husband (*De mala muliere quae dat marito suo cum pugno*). She treated him rudely, but everything ends up happily: when he wanted to kiss her, she punched him on the nose and kissed him in bed (*Quando vult eam osculari, dat ei cum pugno in rostrum et osculatur ad lectum*).[8] But another wife who was a good woman (*mulier bona*) complained that her husband did not love her any more (*conquesta est de marito suo, quod eam non diligeret*).[9] And another woman loved her husband so intensely that she was very jealous: "the jealous wife, when her husband was away, desired longingly to be kissed (*sponsa zelotypa sponsum suum absentem attentissime desiderat osculari*), and sighed frequently because of that, often saying tearfully, 'Quant vendra li dulz, li frant qui mimicer desire tant?' When he came, she kissed him in tears, and God knows that kiss was more precious than a thousand gold pieces (*cum venerit, cum lacrimis osculatur, osculum illud quandoque plus mille aureis appretiatur, Deus scit*).[10] These examples are not taken from royal families, but from among commoners who were less likely to have their marriages arranged. Among the common people there was love between married couples and this was considered to be the norm. In the eyes of preachers who used such examples to encourage virtue, the absence of love was a fault.

Marriage Processes

To all these good or bad examples taken from real life or imagined by the authors, we can add the many matrimonial cases which came before the courts and the details of which were kept in registers which still exist today but which have not been greatly consulted up to now. These texts may be included in monastic literature to the extent that they originate from cathedrals served by monks, which was frequently the case in England. In a communication made at the University of Louvain in 1978, Professor Charles Duggan of London University drew attention to the processes revealed by the papal decretals in the twelfth century of marriage lawsuits brought before the papal court for judgment. Professor Duggan remarks that the decisions are much more human and less rigid than they later became. Such humanity and flexibility were in no way detrimental to principles: the law was applied with justice, compassion, prudence, practical wisdom, and sound common sense, taking into account real persons and situations.[11]

For the immediately following period we still have the records of sentences passed by diocesan courts. The interest presented by this wealth of documentation has been highlighted recently by an authority, M. Sheehan,[12] on the occasion of the excellent study of R. H. Helmholz on the texts of this kind written in England between the end of the thirteenth century and the close of the fifteenth,[13] a period somewhat later than the one we are concerned with here. However, we can assume that the conclusions that emerged could be claimed as accurate for an earlier period and for all countries because the juridical concepts according to which these cases were judged and decided followed a tradition drawn up by lawyers in the twelfth century. How far can works of purely literary value be still utilized as being revealing of social and psychological realities of the Middle Ages? This is a serious question that must be asked when, through the deliberations and declarations of Church courts, so much light has been shed on the intimate relations which existed within marriage, what went on within the nuclear family, the reality of which existed long before our contemporaries coined the phrase. "Analysis by theologians and canonists has established the fundamental role played by the consent of the couple and has denied the fact that the consent of the family and overlord was necessary."[14] But in actual practice, marriages very often had taken place without the presence of witnesses and without therefore having a public character, and also there was no clear-cut distinction between betrothal and marriage. It was only natural that disputes should arise. Divorce proceedings were rare, for generally the courts aimed at reaffirming the marriage and restoring "peace to the household."[15] One of the reasons for the great interest presented by this documentation, is that it informs us not only about noble families— narrations found in courtly hagiography and literature—but about people of humble condition, villeins and serfs. Sheehan concludes that the results of such research lead us to make "a drastic reappraisal of conceptions that have been accepted for too long, a strict criticism of scholars' conclusions, even the greatest among them, which have been put forward previous to these researches."[16] The time has come to challenge historians of literature their erstwhile monopoly of dissertations about love in the Middle Ages. In the future, the canonists should have their say as well.

What do we read in these marriage processes? We find at the beginning of a collection of documents published by Helmholz a striking example: "She said to him: 'I want to tell you something, if you do not mind.' And her husband said: 'Go ahead.' So she continued: 'There is no one in the world I love more than you.' And to that he answered: 'Thank you very much: and it is the same with me, I love you too.' " The editor hastens to add, "Of course, not all processes give such a story. . . ."[17] But we do find love mentioned in other processes. We find the motive of love invoked: *si se invicem diligunt,* if they love one another.[18] Further on in the anthology we read that there was "a woman who did not wish to be separated from the said Thomas Biley but was greatly attached to him (*summe affectat*) and wanted him for her husband."[19] There was a woman of character, a headstrong girl, who "was married for love alone, in opposition to the wishes of her family."[20] There was also a complaint addressed to a girl by a man who languished for love of her, "almost to the point of death."[21] Another plaintiff asks to be allowed to marry the girl he loves, who was called Godlewe (*ad habendum bonum amorem suum*).[22] Lastly, there is this statement, eloquent in its brevity: "a husband should treat his wife with conjugal affection, at table and in bed" (*tam in mensa quam in lecto*).[23] These last words bring us back to the basic reality of love, mentioned at the beginning. The attitude to love in marriage was a traditional one and in the twelfth century it was given new thrust by theologians and canonists. The words of William Durand, a thirteenth-century canonist, can be quoted in conclusion: he "exhorts husbands to treat their wives with all marital affection."[24]

SIX

Cloistral Literature Versus Secular Writings

❧

Courtly Literature and Real Life

The facts and texts that have so far been recalled concern Christian society as a whole. How may this now be situated in the ensemble of courtly literature? It is well known that the formula of "courtly love" is extremely rare. Twelfth-century people scarcely ever used this expression, if at all, but we frequently come across two others: *courtesy* and *fin' amors*. Before showing what these words meant, it will be useful to recall the social setting in which they were used and the underlying realities.

If there was any "courtly love"—even though it may not have gone by that name—it is because there were courts where lovemaking went on. A specific literature was written for the courts or else under their inspiration. Little is known concerning the two hundred or so poets—of whom about twenty were women—who wrote in and for the courtly circles of the twelfth century. It seems that many belonged to the lower nobility, and the courts for which they wrote were not usually of princely rank. The castles in the small provincial towns had something of the nature of *salons,* which people frequented in order to exert and show their talents. Many poets lived wandering, even sometimes very agitated lives in sentimental, financial, or military adventures. One was even given the nickname "Cercamon," which is equivalent to "globe-trotter." Not all remained trouvères or troubadours all their life long. Some ended by settling down, and many seemed to have spent the last and longest period of their lives as happily married men.

Whatever may have been the diversity of family origins or social standing, these poets had in common their talent. This was unequally divided out, which helps to understand why there was sometimes rivalry and jealously among them, and accounts for the fact that they readily employed irony about one another. They sometimes let out pent-up feelings of resentment, even going so far as to insult one another.

Courtesy (*curialitas, cortezia*) was first a sociological fact, the province of people who lived at court. It then became a character trait, the charm of politeness, "civility," and even of "virtue." But "to make courtesy" sometimes means nothing other than "to make love." From certain texts we can draw up a complex doctrine and code of courteous love. Historians have not yet elucidated the real contents of these,[1] but we may well assume that things were as Professor C. Brooke depicts them: "In its literary developments and in certain of its lineaments this literary fashion was deliberately intended to contradict, or else to parody, the facts of social life."[2] Thus, it was far from being a reflection of real life. It rather shows what it was not like.

One of the manifestations of courtesy was occasionally the *fin' amors,* a fine love which, though it may sometimes have been refined, was always concerned basically with the flesh. Some romances, for example, *Erec and Enide* by Chrétien de Troyes, were merely in praise of marital love, excluding any sense of guilt in the pleasures enjoyed. In other texts, refined love consisted of making love to someone other than one's lawful married partner; or else in making love in such a way as to avoid procreation. But there was not necessarily an opposition between *fin' amors* and conjugal love. Had this been the case, we may wonder whether this degradation of Christian love would have had any real impact on the people of the times apart from the enjoyment of writing or listening to love adventures.[3] Had it been a real danger for many people, then surely reformers like Bernard of Clairvaux and others would have attacked it openly, as they refuted the Cathars in the field of doctrine, and the various moral deviations in Church and society. Perhaps the ambiguities of this artificial literary production for the use of a small social elite was just one more indication of the mystery enshrouding the activity of love. It must be remembered that courtly literature recommended moderation (*mezura*), exactly as did Saint Augustine and the twelfth-century Schoolmen, so that passion may be controlled.

When Erec's love for Enide becomes excessive and has to be reoriented, it is his wife and the Christian community who remind him of his duty.

It is perhaps because of the positive values of this secular literature that so many churchmen were able to make such frank use of the symbolism of human love when they wanted to exalt the love that all men must have for God. Nowhere does Hugh of Saint-Victor speak of a human love affair with such frankness, precision, and at the same time with such poetry and delicacy, as he does when writing on the Virginity of Mary. We can say the same about the treatise by Richard of Saint-Victor *On the Four Degrees of Passionate Love;* about the many and sublime hymns to love which give such beauty to Saint Bernard's masterpiece, the *Sermons on the Song of Songs;* about the hymns and writings of Saint Hildegard of Bingen, and of so many other texts of spiritual writers. To the problems of love in marriage, theologians and canonists had found immediate solutions. But it was the task of spiritual masters—some of whom were also Schoolmen and canonists—to give a higher presentation of the same realities, in direct relation to the union with God.

In connection with Saint Bernard, Jean Deroy, who is familiar with the works of the troubadours contemporary with Saint Bernard or writing before his time, has said about the "erotic or nuptial allegory": "The troubadours and Saint Bernard can in fact go far along the road together; when the troubadours come to a halt, Saint Bernard flies up to those heights which are beyond the reach of the troubadours and of which they can do no more than ape a description." He suggests that themes and vocabulary which troubadours take as an end in themselves are for Bernard only a springboard: "This springboard is useful for him to reach his end. Thus these strangers have become rivals! Give me a hundred pages in which to quote from the works of Saint Bernard, the beautiful things, the findings, the riches, and sometimes those artifices which were in those times otherwise esteemed than today. Five pages would be enough for the first troubadours! Because there is not one expression of love from which Saint Bernard recoils." And after having quoted a passage from Sermon 14 on the Song in which the vocabulary is so precise that is hardly acceptable otherwise than in Latin, the same historian adds: "It is more realistic than the troubadours. . . ."[4]

It is refreshing to read what another modern scholar stated during a symposium held at Louvain.[5] He pointed out that in the twelfth century, love in marriage was the normal thing. In a recent publication he reminds us that the lays of Marie de France do not give an unfavorable view of marriage. In such lays, marriage is considered as something so worthy that, whenever possible, unlawful unions are broken up and give place to lawful weddings.[6] A little further on, this same writer again reminds us that it would be false to imagine that marriage is contested and that extramarital relations are constantly valorized. Things were not as simple as that. In the texts under consideration, marriage is something safe and even occasionally a refuge. Neither adultery nor concubinage are unprudently exhibited.[7] It must not be forgotten, however, that such reflections concern a particular kind of literature: the lays. But they ought to rouse our curiosity as to whether other forms of literature considered marital love or extramarital relations as being the normal thing. And in the event of extramarital love, the role of the hermit in the *Tristan* of Béroul and other writings was not to condemn but rather to awaken, at least in the conscience, the awareness of what would have been the better thing. And it does seem to have been one of the functions of monastic literature on divine and human love, at a period when more than at any other time in the West love literature was being developed, to rouse the Christian conscience to what was right in matters of love.

Andrew's *De Amore:* the Antimodel

In the present context it is appropriate that the *Three Books on Love* should be briefly mentioned again. They are now generally attributed to Andrew the Chaplain.[8] We still sometimes read statements about this author which do not conform to the findings of the most recent research work in this field. It is said, for instance, that he had great influence from the last quarter of the twelfth century onward. Or he is said to be the typical representative, the perfect theorist of courtly love, and, according to this, the pleasure of love, love itself can only find satisfaction in adultery. It has already been pointed out above that this last assumption is unfounded: there was no uniform conception of courtly love, let alone a single and dogmatic teaching. Furthermore, marital love could quite well be a *fin' amors*. As to the immediate and widespread success of this treatise, we have no clear evidence on the subject. On the contrary, it seems certain that it had fewer copyists and readers in the twelfth century than printers and translators in the twentieth.

The author is named Andrew in only nine of the manuscripts dating before the year 1500. Elsewhere he is called Alan, Pogius, and especially Galter.[9] The place where the text was composed was not Champagne, and it is now confirmed that the author was not connected with the court of Troyes. He wrote at Paris and not in a small provincial court.[10] The royal court in which he wrote had chancelleries employing a large staff of clerics who understood Latin. His "first readership must surely have been chiefly among clerks rather than aristocracy, clerks eager for gossip and scandal, true or invented, about the great and their way of life." This treatise is "an essentialy clerical performance."[11] It was composed between 1174 and 1238. It was long thought that the date of composition was somewhere near the year 1180. But it is now admitted that it could have been written "at some time in the first four decades of the thirteenth century."[12]

The treatise was not widely diffused. There were only twenty-eight Latin manuscripts of the whole text or fragments. One or perhaps two of them are of the thirteenth century, three are of the fourteenth, nineteen of the fifteenth. The French translation dates from 1290. It was translated into Catalan and Italian in the fourteenth century. The two German texts are of the fifteenth century.[13] Thus the conclusion is clear: all the statements so far made on the influence of the text on its times are unfounded.[14] The golden ages of the *De amore* were the fourteenth, the fifteenth, and now the twentieth century. This observation allows the suggestion that the popularity which this text enjoys, even up to our own day, among medievalists[15] permits the inference that it was the same in the Middle Ages.

We may even lawfully think that the *De amore* is a good proof of what real love was, insofar as it portrays just the opposite: far from being a great theorist of courtly love, Andrew is the theorist of false love, love which is no longer conformable to its end,[16] and even of the absence of love. He is a theorist, not in the sense that he was a master teaching a sure doctrine, but by way of contrast and negatively. His writing is a parody. There exist parodies which use grammar and logic for erotic purposes.[17] The treatise of Saint Bernard on humility is perhaps parodied.[18] But certainly the *quaestiones,* the *disputationes,* and the *summae* of the Schoolmen writing at the close of the twelfth century and during the first half of the thirteenth are. That Andrew's text is a parody is clearly shown by the plan and the vocabulary.[19] We find the words *treatise, doctrine,* and *knowledge* mentioned in the same sequence as that used by Saint Bernard. The conclusion is as emphatic as could be: "Our treatise, if you will only study it, and take pains carefully to examine it, applying to it all the intelligence of which your mind is capable, if you seek to put into practice and carry out its doctrine, you will have clear knowledge of this same with manifest satisfaction. . . ."[20] This cleric, whoever he was, must have had great fun laughing at his masters! But who, among laymen not initiated to the jargon of the schools, could have appreciated the irony of the text? It even contains a parody of the formularies for letters as they were generally used, particularly in the chancelleries: almost as if it were possible to make love by letter. . . .[21]

In short, the author of the *De amore* is making fun of the entire milieu in which he lives. He is truly the antimodel of love in the twelfth century. And in particular he is the antimodel of one of the major trends of the new monastic milieux working to abolish class distinction between nobles and villeins in religious communities.[22] The *De amore* confirms the importance which secular society attributed to social barriers and against which theologians and spiritual writers reacted in the name of charity.[23]

The Contribution of the Monastic Twelfth Century

To conclude: we have a glimpse of how the contribution of cloistral authors fits into the literary history of conjugal love. There had long been in the Christian West a living and lived tradition of love in marriage. It was based on the ancient notions of marital affection enlivened and enriched by the Christian conception of charity. By reason of various historical circumstances and different cultural influences, this tradition contained a certain number of ambiguous and obscure points, and in the twelfth century it confronted the faithful, and consequently pastors too, with new and hitherto unthought-of problems. The canonists and theologians put forth solutions based on ethical and doctrinal principles, and these were developed and explicated in spiritual literature. The basic principles were protracted and projected ideally in hagiographic models. They were thus mirrored in literature intended to put doctrine within reach of the general public. Such writings reveal the uniformity of the prevailing religious culture: over and beyond the variety of literary genres and the diversity of the milieux for which they were written, we notice that there is constant reference to the basic realities assumed.

From the Carolingian period onward, family ethics were gradually elaborated on the basis of Christian principles concerning conjugal fidelity, the equality of rights and duties between husband and wife, chastity, that is to say, moderation and reserve in the use of marriage and indulgence whenever there was lack of "measure." Most of the theorists were clerics, generally not monks. In certain "mirrors (*specula*) of spouses," we notice that the traditional severity in such matters, which resulted from the influence of Saint Jerome, began to soften a little and there was more leniency. However, the major effort of pastoral reflection aimed at restoring and strengthening the family as a basic cell of society. The pastoral writings were intended on the whole for nobles, around whom not only was society organized but who were also its protectors and its models.[24] At the same period Saint Benedict of Aniane taught the "love of friendship": this is "freely bestowed . . . a friend must be loved gratuitously, for himself and for nothing else."[25]

In the following generations, the influence of the *specula* waned a little until the second half of the eleventh century. With the Gregorian reform the necessity was felt to update the doctrine on marriage. However, the revision was for the greater part the work of austere monks who often instinctively took refuge behind the authority of Saint Jerome. This was not always so, for some of the revisers were ardent mystics who extolled the free character of love for God and men. The most illustrious among such mystics was Jean de Fécamp. As did many of his contemporaries, he composed for monks and laymen, and especially for women, texts which enjoyed great popularity, were widely read, and became a source of inspiration for other writings. He differed from his peers in that he wrote with more exquisite psychological insight.[26] Such spiritual literature furthered the progress of the doctrine of love in two complementary literary fields, that of monastic love, i.e., the doctrine elaborated by monastic writers, and that of courtly love.[27]

From the beginning of the twelfth century we notice a relaxation, so to speak, of the severity inspired by Saint Jerome. In relation to this, the words *sexual liberation* have been pronounced. But it seems more exact to describe it as a literature concerned with ascetical principles to the detriment of an equitable and adequate consideration of personal problems. Generally, however, the individual member of society came to enjoy the same concern as the social structure which is the family. We notice an evolution; a sort of double process which leads to what might be described as both the particularization and the popularization of previously existing ideas reserved to a social elite. The love which married couples should have for one another was subjected to critical analysis, and at the same time the teaching which had hitherto been dispensed to a princely and noble aristocracy was generalized and applied to all other classes of society: the lower nobility, the middle class, and villeins.

Thus we see that the preexisting principles of ethics and custom gave rise to a new literature tinged with psychology, fresh spiritual teaching, and a poetic of love. Monastic writers made no small contribution to all this literary production. Generally speaking, monks did not elaborate a spirituality of marriage. That was not their business. But they supposed that such a spirituality existed, and they indirectly spread it abroad in every milieu by exposing their own thought on the matter. Monks do not necessarily always state that their way of treating the subject, which is always directed to increasing love for God, can only be lived in celibacy. On the whole, they do not exclude and they even explicitly admit the possibility for married people to live the ideal of union with God. In monastic writings in which conjugal union is transformed, sublimated, and, so to speak, retrieved as a metaphor of union with God, then the lovemaking between married persons is acknowledged and given an honorable place in cloistral literature. Conjugal love is presented less as an obligation than as a verification: it is a fact before being a duty. This does not mean that it is always easy. Married life has its temptations, which are overcome by the help of God's grace. Saint Bernard recognizes such temptations as being specific to human beings as rational creatures able to realize that there exist good things even greater than those they already possess: hence the temptation: desire for a greater good. "For example, the man who has a pretty wife, looks with desire at a prettier woman."[28] Therein lies the danger of straying from the right way. Such is the "law of cupidity," which, in the domain of marriage, as in every other, must be replaced by a "Law of discipline" through the instrumentality of the "curb of temperance."[29]

Occasionally secular, and especially courtly, literature sought to justify extraconjugal love relations, which, from the Christian point of view, are abnormal. There was never any need to justify conjugal love between married persons, for this is the normal thing. However, like everything else which is normal, it may easily come to be taken for granted: an ordinary, commonplace event emptied of its stimulus. For this reason, the fidelity of such love is to be safeguarded by the asceticism of moderation. Such measure is exacting, but, as has already been remarked, so is the code of courtly love. And though the demands of courtly love differed from the requirements of Christian ethics, they were sometimes more difficult to observe, if ever they were.

Finally, it must be noticed that generally speaking, and especially in its most illustrious representatives, cloistral literature on marriage and love allows us to correct and to complete the image of women which secular literature of the times very often sketched. Nonverified commonplaces about women are related to other such statements about marriage. In profane literature we read occasionally that marriage, far from implying love, even excludes it. Consequently love finds satisfaction only in adultery, and a wife who is not loved can only be spurned. As to the antifeminism which is sometimes attributed to Saint Bernard and other writers, the texts prove that it is fictitious.[30] Generally it is the secular writers like John of Salisbury or Andrew the Chaplain who are misogynic. They follow in the steps of the pre-Christian satirists from whom they take their inspiration. Monastic writers, if they are truly theologians, versed in the Bible, especially the New Testament, never elaborate antifeminist doctrine. In practice they advised men who had freely chosen celibacy to be reserved with women. And, of course, they shared with their contemporaries certain cultural attitudes.

When dealing with questions concerning marriage and women, we must be careful to avoid generalizations advanced on the evidence of a restricted number of documents. This is true for the "ideal" woman, the dream come true, and for expressions such as that which describes woman as a "bag of filth." An authority on Islam has had the courage to declare: "It is the same in Arabic poetry as in Occitan poetry: it is to be wondered whether the woman who is thus sung really exists."[31] Between the nun and the adulteress stands the faithful wife; between the woman who is sung and the woman who is despised stands the real woman, who was, normally, the loved wife of an equally loved husband.

SEVEN

Saint Bernard and the Metaphor of Love

❖

More than any other monk in the twelfth century, Saint Bernard used the allegory of love in his teaching on the Christian mysteries. Is it possible, we may ask, to have an insight as to the workings of this metaphor in his psychology and his theology? To answer this question we must first verify to what extent the comparison he draws between human love and other realities is founded. What exactly is the love he considers? How does this love fit into the context of his times? The careful perusal of the eighty-six *Sermons on the Song of Songs* and a selection of a few other characteristic traits in his works will help us to answer these questions and suggest parallels with other writers.

The Basic Fact

Love is Bernard's frame of reference for allegory. But what sort of love? Love between whom? There is nothing in Saint Bernard's early writings which provides an element of response to these queries. His first works do not deal with love at all. "Letter 11" and the treatise *On the Necessity of Loving God (De diligendo Deo)*, though they contain a few reminiscences and quotations of the Song, offer no definite commentary. However, the *Sermons on the Song of Songs* states without any ado the basic fact upon which are founded the poetic and mystical elevations of these sermons, and that from the very first pages. The vocabulary of love is used repeatedly throughout the whole of the introductory sermon, which speaks of marriage, wedding, embracings.

There is mention of a bridegroom, and of a bride who knows how to make love because she is nubile. Bernard aims at teaching men, readers and listeners, who are no longer novices in the spiritual life for, as he points out, the epithalamium, the wedding song of the biblical Canticle of Canticles is not to be put indiscriminately into everyone's hands.[1]

Saint Bernard declares that he is addressing his monks. These were more or less young adults who had already had some love experience before their conversion and entry into the monastic state.[2] The abbot reminds them of their secular days and alludes to the impressions engraved in their memories: "Among those who wear the religious habit and have made religious profession, there are some who remember—and they even boast impertinently about it—certain bad actions which they committed in the past. They are proud of having courageously struck with the sword or of their agility in literary jousts and of other wordly vanities to which they gave themselves. . . . All these things come back to the memory and they either repent of having done them or else swell up with pride."[3] An allusion made by Beranger to Bernard's own youth hints that "literary" jousts were not all of a scholarly or a doctrinal nature. The competition sometimes consisted in proving that one could write more spicy verse than another. . . .[4] It is these still-vivid memories which provide the background for the images Bernard evokes and interprets. It is a delicate matter to go into details in any other tongue than Latin, which, even at the time Bernard composed his sermons, was already to a certain extent conventional. This sacred and perhaps already dying language served to drape and cover up the nakedness of cruder details in poetic elegance. However, in spite of the delicate nature of the task, literary scientific probity forbids us to pass them over in silence.

The biblical Song of Songs opens with clear mention of a kiss, and Bernard, too, uses this first metaphor. But the "contact of the lips" is only a symbol of a more englobing metaphor: embrace in love.[5] The kiss is first described as a touching of the lips which pour out and reciprocally exchange something desirable.[6] It is then described as the initial act, which, between lovers, generally ends in consummated embrace.[7] After the kiss of the lips, the bride becomes a mother: she conceives and her breasts swell with milk and if they are pressed, they will nurture a suckling.[8] Accordingly, perfumed and milk-laden breasts are more fructuous than the first embrace,[9] at least in the fiancée who is intimately aware that she is no longer a child.[10]

Other remindful mentions of the kiss conjure up more vividly before our eyes what was merely suggested in the first image: "When we are about to embrace, do we not bring our mouths together?"[11] Notice that Bernard speaks in the plural, which indicates clearly enough that he is alluding to an experience about which everyone knows. Again, he says: "The kiss is a mouth to mouth: it draws two people together in embrace and union";[12] "To exchange a kiss, the lips of two mouths press together."[13]

The text of the Song of Songs says simply, "Let him kiss me with the kiss of his lips," but Bernard's commentary is evocative of greater detail and suggests with a fair amount of precision the lovemaking implied. It is as if the value of the allegory depended upon the realism of the comparative term, and one would be inclined to think that the logic of Bernard's theological developments required a striking representation of both the symbol and its object. And, as we know, it is true that the aptness of a metaphor and its lawful use in a given context do depend very strictly upon the neatness with which the original sense of the basic fact fits the figured, transposed one. Bernard conformed to the laws governing this literary genre and was greatly rewarded for his pains, as we shall see.

One of the things which strikes us when we read his texts is that his description of the clasp (*amplexio*) or the loving embrace (*amplexus*) is even more precise than his account of the kiss, and this whether he is suggesting the prelude or the actual embrace. He depicts the bride daring to enter the bridegroom's chamber: she bursts in upon him, heedless of reserve, without restraint. The bridegroom recognizes her and takes her to himself in loving embrace entailing warmth, pressure, and friction, union, effusion, reception.[14] And Bernard repeats, "Alone, within the nuptial chamber, the bride and bridegroom enjoy mutual loving embrace."[15] In sentences such as this one, the words are very realistic. But they are biblical and this gives them an added mysterious charm. Though they are compact in meaning, they are not unduly stressed, and if Saint Bernard's use of them is compared with the use made by certain erotic poems written at the same period where almost each term is provocatively descriptive as if the writer intended to stir up delight in the mind of his readers, the difference will easily be noticed.[16] There is nothing similar to these erotic poems in Bernard's text. It suffices to interject a few other biblical words charged with a spiritual sense and the concrete words of the fleshly realities rise to the same lofty level. The liberty, the spontaneity of the bride's inrushing, is the freedom of the Holy Spirit. The warmth of the embrace is an effect of the burning of Christ's Spirit of love. We see this in another place where Bernard's inserts, between the "touch of the lips" and the "undistinguishable mingling" (*indiscreta commixtio*), an "outpouring of joys" (*infusio gaudiorum*), and it is these last two words which at once raise the mind on high. The choice of words used, the musicality of the phrases, the literary beauty snatch all these images away from the sensual sphere. And Bernard maintains this sublimity throughout every one of the eighty-six sermons. In the last one he thrice mentions the intimacy, the secrecy of the bed at night.[17]

Another element in the metaphor used by Saint Bernard is the dialogue between the lovers. They first look upon each other because the gaze is a sign of love (*aspectus, indices amoris*). Then the bridegroom calls the fiancée his "love" (*illam amicam nuncupat*). He says, over and over again, that she is beautiful (*pulchram pronuntiat, pulchram iterat*). And she in return utters the same sweet words to him (*eandem ab illa vicissim recipiens*). Love is now confirmed (*amoris confirmatio*).[18] "The bridegroom is in love and continuously speaks words of love: he calls her 'my dove, my very own.' " And now, what she once begged from him, he ardently expects from her: he longs for her to gaze upon him and to speak to him! He behaves still like a shy bridegroom, one who would blush to love her in public. He decides to enjoy her in some hidden place, in the cleft of the rock, in the covert of the cliff. And here again, because of the Latinized Hebraisms in which they are clothed, the words, though still telling of stark reality, become wreathed in mystery. "Imagine the conversation! The bridegroom says to her, 'Have no fear, my love, that the work in the vineyard where I invite you will hinder our lovemaking.' But surely this *negotium amoris* is quite opposed to *otium*, leisure, free time? No! it will not even interrupt it. Even in the vineyard there will be time for that which we both sigh after: *id quod pariter optamus*."[19] The text does not tell us what *id* refers to here. In such language, spangled as it is with words from the Vulgate which are often hazy, vague, mysterious, the actual consummation of love is never mentioned in overbold or common terms; it is always wrapped in poetry.

This intimate, ardent love is exchanged between two people. But it is not always very clear who they are. The loving embrace described implies the presence of a bride and a bridegroom in the strictest sense of these words as distinct from the baser activity between a man and a prostitute.[20] Previous texts are more explicit and there is no hesitation as to who is who: Bernard is dealing with conjugal love. This affection (*affectio*) does not exist in other social categories. We do not find it among slaves, mercenaries, hired servants, disciples, or sons. This affection of love (*affectio amoris*) is "specific to the bride and bridegroom." The implication is that "Between them, they have everything in common, nothing belongs personally to either one or the other, there is no division." This community of life contains elements of the social, physical, and affective orders: "There is one heirship, one house, one table, one bed, one flesh." There we recognize all that is contained in "marital affection." And Scripture confirms us in this: "A man shall leave his father and his mother and be joined to his wife." Consequently, there can be no doubt that the word *sponsa* is synonymous with *uxor*. The text continues in support of this statement: all that is said here is said "specifically of the betrothed ones," "she is called a bride."[21] Nothing suggests that this love is the whim of a passing moment.

Such marital love is chaste and is exclusive of adultery. It is permanent and free from selfish interest. The bride "loves chastely, she who seeks the one she loves, and him alone."[22] It is only this sort of love which has access to intimacy (*accessus ad intima*).[23] So, the basic fact, the foundation of the metaphor is indeed marriage, and at last the word is pronounced: "Fleshly marriage unites the two in one flesh. . . ."[24] There is absolutely no mention of lovers (*amatores*), everything is focused on the bride's husband (*vir tuus*).[25] Matrimony, which Bernard mentions so clearly here, is not to be found in the Song. He added it in conformity with the cultural and social structures of his own times. Throughout all his sermons he draws a constant contrast between the "bride," her young maiden companions, and other women. She alone shares her husband's house (*domestica*); she alone is his darling, his cherished one. She alone is found to be pleasing and is introduced into his chamber,[26] reserved for her alone, and she alone enjoys secretly his presence.[27] Neither the queen nor the concubines, nor the other young maidens mentioned by the Song, are thus privileged. Everything pivots round the one and only bride.[28]

The text of the Song of Songs is vague and does not leave room for clear and sure mention of the married state of the two lovers. However, the opening verses are clear enough and they subtend all Bernard's sermons. In the seven final ones he mentions the spousal bond again quite distinctly. He mentions the "affinity" of "the habits and love of the two spouses" (*more et amore sponsorum*),[29] the marriage (*nuptiae*), the social contract (*inire foedus societatis*), which lead the bride to "carry with the king the sweet yoke of love."[30] "Such conformity marries her to the bridegroom" (*maritat*). It implies mutual approach, union, reciprocal solicitation, and desire. The contract is a loving embrace (*contractus, immo complexus*) between equals because, from now on, the two partners are "bride and bridegroom."[31] Saint Matthew is brought in as a witness: "Because of that, a man shall leave his father and his mother and be joined to his wife."[32] This informs us as to the total content of the union (*adhaerebit*),[33] which means a contract and an embrace in marital love. The specific traits of such love are fidelity and reciprocity (*amoris vicem requirit et fidem*).[34] The words *to espouse, consent* have a very precise meaning. In the last completed sermon, Bernard makes a final statement on fleshly union (*carnale connubium*), consecrated by the "wedding." Love brings the two lovers together and their commitment to fidelity marries them: *amor conciliat, professio*[35] *maritat*. And again Saint Matthew is quoted. We find the verb *to unite* (*adhaerere*) used three times in relation to the "bride" (*coniux*), marriage (*maritalis*), and the notion of fidelity and fecundity by which the bride becomes a mother. As is clearly seen, the frame of reference for the metaphor is indeed the fleshly love existing between married people. We find the same frame in the *Brief Commentary on the Song* composed by William of Saint-Thierry, probably in collaboration with Saint Bernard: "The bridegroom and the bride according to the flesh show each other mutual respect. This is what Rebecca did when she ran to meet her new bridegroom."[36]

The consideration of certain antimodels of this union, which, according to Saint Bernard, is normal between married lovers, brings us to the same conclusion. In Jungian psychology the "shadow" is the other side of reality and makes it stand out in its essential being, and we find something comparable in the *Sermons on the Song*. The direct opposite to matrimonial union is prostitution, adultery, and the free union advanced by the Rhineland heretics.[37] Prostitution will be the subject of the next chapter. Adultery, also called fornication, consists in a woman leaving her husband, to whom she has promised fidelity, and going off with lovers. After a time of infidelity, she comes back to her husband, whom she loves and who, she knows, loves her. She takes up with him once more the normal relations which should exist between a man and his wife (*vir et uxor*). These are mentioned by Jeremiah the prophet.[38]

In refuting the Rhineland heretics, Bernard takes the opportunity for reiterating the facts of conjugal union. The major evil was that "women leave their husbands and men leave their wives." Who is this woman? Where does she come from? Is she your wife? No! they say.[39] For them the marriage act with wives is a shameful thing,[40] whereas in fact it is only honest if carried out between husband and wife.[41] Bernard makes an energetic defense in favor of marriage: "Take away from the Church honorable marriage and you also do away with the stainless marriage bed."[42] The contrast between the clefts in the rock where bride and bridegroom seek intimacy in fidelity, and those caverns where the heretics conceal their infidelity and their licentiousness is very striking.[43] Such defense in favor of sexual congress in marriage (*maritalis copula*) establishes once and for all that Bernard and all monks considered marriage to be the normal state of union between a man and a woman. Any other union, subject to change and caprice, is absolutely rejected.

Metaphorical Transpositions:
Love within the Trinity

St. Bernard draws a close parallel between "fleshly union" (*carnale connubium*) and "spiritual marriage" (*spirituale matrimonium*).[44] The analogy is based on a constant and realistic description of conjugal love. It is used to express a theological thought which is sound to the extent that this basic fact is accurate. He maneuvers the transposition from one register to another by situating it on three different planes. First, love between the three Divine Persons, then between the Word and the Humanity of Christ, and finally the love exchanged between God, Christ, his Church, and each single member of the Church.

Rather than innovate, Bernard renovates. He gives already existing facts new and unexpected expression in developments determinative of any future evolution. Thus, his contribution in this field of metaphorical transposition can be correctly evaluated only if it is set against the background of tradition. So it is that we find in the fifth century, long before him, Saint Fulgentius of Ruspe, following Saint Ambrose and Saint Augustine, applied to the Holy Spirit the image of the human breath exhaled when bride and bridegroom kiss.[45] And the Risen Christ himself breathed on his Apostles and thus communicated to them his Holy Spirit.[46] It is from then onward that we can trace "the avatars of the conjugal and family analogy in the history of the theology of the Trinity."[47] This symbolism dropped out of use after the twelfth century because the Scholastics were less in favor of it, a fact which was due principally to the devaluation, if we may so say, of the role of womankind. However, the idea that "the property of the Holy Spirit is to be an inter-Person"[48] lingered on. The marriage metaphor applied to the Trinity was taken up again in the nineteenth century by Scheeben, and, nearer to our own day, by Heribert Möhler,[49] Pierre Bellego,[50] Adrienne von Speyer,[51] and others. The metaphor is part of a more comprehensive fact: friendship, of which conjugal love is a privileged form.[52] These very few elements concerning the historical and doctrinal context show that Bernard, though he is traditional, is also creative. A precise summary of his teaching has recently been the object of an informed study.[53] But this merits more careful examination and is worth expounding at some length.

The essentials of Saint Bernard's doctrine are contained in the eighth of the *Sermons on the Song*. The conciseness of its phrases, the precision of the images, especially that of the kiss, and the appositeness of the theological application call forth our admiration. The entire sermon speaks of love: in God, each Person embraces the Other in preferential love, hugs him to himself in affection. "This exchange of knowledge and love between the Engendering and the Engendered, what is it if not a very sweet and very secret kiss?"[54] Bernard identifies this kiss with the Risen Christ's breathing upon his disciples when he imparted the Spirit to the nascent Church: "The kiss is not his physical breath, but the indivisible Spirit who is given in this breath, so that all might understand that he proceeds equally from the Lord and from the Father like to some kiss common to Embracer and Embraced. . . . It is the Father who embraces, the Son is embraced, and the Spirit is the Kiss, the untroubled peace and the undivided unity of the Father and the Son."[55] The sermon goes on to develop this idea that "relevation is made through the Kiss, that is, the Holy Spirit."[56] "When the Father kisses the Son, he reveals himself to him, exhales and (as the technical word says) spirates in loving embrace of mutual love and reciprocal acceptance."[57] Life in the Trinity is "one eternal and blessed loving embrace." The Holy Spirit is that kiss of the lips which the Father bestows upon the Son. And for the Father this kiss of the lips is to be in the Son. For the Son it is to be in the Father.[58] The preceding precise descriptions of the bestowal of a kiss were a fitting preparation for this precise theology: Father and Son are united as equals, they embrace as equals, the mouth of the one is pressed to the mouth of the other at an equal height.[59] Thus the symbolism of the kiss first expresses the unity of the Godhead in the self-sufficient Trinity of Persons. Secondly, it illustrates the distinction and the equality of the three Persons in one God and neatly describes the order existing among them and which governs the order in which they unite. This is exactly what the Latin theological tradition calls the order of processions.

The doctrine of this sermon is summed up in Sermon 89: *On Different Matters, De diversis.* "The Son is the Father's mouth . . . . This reciprocal revelation of the Father and the Son only happens in the Holy Spirit. Thus, if the Father and the Son kiss each other, this kiss is surely none other than the Holy Spirit."[60] In these texts we are struck by the realism of the imagery, the logic of the allegorical transpositions, and the originality of the use made of an age-old theme familiar to many different traditions for hundreds, perhaps thousands of years. For, it must be realized, the symbolism of the kiss is not confined to a single culture. It is universal, a sort of archetype.[61] We find it frequently mentioned in the Old Testament and in other religious traditions, such as Hinduism.[62] In Christianity, the Latin Fathers were the first to exploit the gospel image of the breath. The notion of communion in love was contributed by Saint Augustine: Fulgentius brought in the sword, which is the Word proceeding from the mouth of God and deeply penetrating souls. It is interesting to notice in passing that Saint Bernard quotes Fulgentius when, in the *Sermons on the Song,* he refutes Gilbert Porreta in connection with his teaching on the Trinity.[63] It is clear that for Saint Bernard the kiss signifies the act of love exchanged between bride and bridegroom. It supposes that they are equals. The bride is not a mere passive partner, she is equal to the bridegroom and takes an active part in the kissing. Furthermore, the kiss is common to both. It is evident from all that has gone before that the nuptial allegory very fittingly serves as a symbol descriptive of the life within the Trinity.

Christ the Mediator

This last statement is applicable, too, to the mystery of the Incarnation. Bernard uses several different allegories here. For example, in his treatise *On Consideration, De consideratione,* he compares the hypostatic union, the nature of God and the nature of man united in the Person of the Word made flesh, to the union of yeast in the bread which it leavens. In some manuscripts this passage is called a parable.[64] In the *Sermons on the Song,* the union in Christ of the divine and the human nature is symbolized from the beginning by the kiss. Bernard states the fact in the following words, "To be kissed with the kiss of the lips is the singular privilege of the humanity assumed by the Word."[65] The explanation follows: "Reflect carefully: the lips which kiss are the Word which assumes and the kissed is the flesh assumed. As for the kiss, bestowed simultaneously by kisser and kissed, it is the Person in whom both the one and the other are found. He is the man Jesus Christ, the mediator between God and men."[66] Thus, we see, just as the kiss with its three inseparable elements first symbolized the three Persons in one God, so now it symbolizes the two natures in the unity of Christ, the Word made flesh. And once again it is the accuracy of the basic fact which permits precision in the theological application.

Bernard goes on to tell us how in Christ there is union yet distinction between the humanity and the divinity. "The lips of the Word press the human nature, and in this way God is united to man in whom henceforth dwells all the fullness of the Godhead." This alliance between God and man is described by a term related to the one used for the marriage contract, *foedus matrimonii:* "This alliance of the two natures adapts the human to the divine."[67] Saint Bernard continues in the same vein until he concludes that in this case and in this context "the kiss is none other than the Mediator."[68]

Union of the Word with the Church

Lastly, the conjugal metaphor lends itself to the expression of the union which exists between Christ and his Church. The Church herself is the communion between souls. Both she and each individual soul are symbolic, the one of the other, because they are inclusive of each other. And here again we are in the presence of three realities which, though distinct, are united: the Church, the individual soul, and the love which unites them. The love is symbolized by active communion in the love act. In the glory of the afterlife, but already here below, we are each one with the Church in the clinging embrace of love. This expression is particularly strong because it means the total embrace, full and complete union. Saint Bernard does not hesitate to use such forceful terms if they can serve his purpose and by their vigor conjure up for his readers and his audience something of the truth of such a mysterious reality so difficult to translate into human language. Every word counts in this sentence concerning the Church: "We possess all that fully and entirely, and there is nothing contradictory in saying that at the same time each one participates individually."[69]

All that has been mentioned above in connection with the bridegroom's lovemaking—looks, words, acts, and so forth[70]—is now applied to the relations existing between the Word and the soul. "The Spirit is the Word, and the Spirit is also the soul. They have a single language when they speak to each other and so prove that they are present one to the other."[71] The looks, words and signs of love unite three distinct but united realities: the Word, the bride who answers and corresponds, and the grace he pours out into her.[72] Further on this mystery is described in terms of love: "There is not simply one soul, there are many gathered together in one Church, embraced as a single bride." As we can hardly fail to remark, the basic fact is always marriage, unique and faithful. "She is most dear to him, she does not unite with another bridegroom, and he does not give way to another bride. With such an aspiring lover, her daring knows no limits."[73]

In the life to come, this mystery will be fully accomplished and revealed. Then "there will be union, mutual vision, mutual love, full knowledge, clear vision, firm union, undivided society. And the Bridegroom will rejoice over his bride, knowing her and known by her, loving her and being loved by her."[74] In the last completed sermon, Bernard brings the analogy of conjugal love to its term, fecundity: the bride becomes a mother. A play on words shows how this happens: *frui Verbo, fructificans Verbo,* which might tentatively be translated as "to enjoy the society of the Word bears fruit to the Word."[75]

In this ecclesial application of the conjugal metaphor, the symbol is no longer the kiss alone, but every sign of love, in particular the meeting of the eyes. For example, when he mentions the love that the Church has for Jesus crucified as she contemplates his pierced side from which flows the stream of grace allowing her to share in his risen glory,[76] Bernard says that the bride's face, turned towards the glory of God, gazes upon her Bridegroom's face, longs to look upon him, and consequently also desires to hear his voice.[77] With a string of biblical quotations Bernard is able to play variations on the themes of the "seeing" and the "hearing" of the bride and the Bridegroom.[78] Elsewhere, in one of his letters, he speaks of the bride as the beloved whose beauty is desired by the Bridegroom: it is this beauty with which he himself is clothed. In his marvelous condescension he has united with the bride in a chaste and indissoluble embrace so that they are now two in one flesh, they who, one day, will be two in one spirit.[79] The Church will be his perfect bride in the glory of the afterlife. But even now she is wedded to him as is a bride to her husband.

At this point Bernard juggles two texts which he brings together in another place as well.[80] The first comes from Genesis (2: 24) and is cited in the Gospel of Saint Matthew: "And the two shall become one flesh." The second is in 1 Corinthians: "He who is joined to the Lord becomes one spirit with him." In the verse just before this one Saint Paul says, "He who joins himself to a prostitute becomes one body with her." Thus, the allegory is evident. In the first case we have an example of what Saint Bernard calls "conjugal unity," in which the two cease to be two and become one flesh.[81] This is the "fleshly union between a man and his wife, as it is written, 'They shall be two in one flesh.' "[82] In the second case we have an example of the union with God by the Holy Spirit. The first is a metaphor for the second, and this latter is the fullness of the first because union was established on earth between the Word-Bridegroom and the Church-Bride.[83] The Latin word (adhaerere) which constantly recurs in these biblical quotations inspiring Saint Bernard means, in the strongest sense of the term, loving embrace. Sometimes it is used to signify, symbolically, spiritual union, and at other times it is used antithetically with an end to stressing the strictly spiritual nature of the union described: "This mutual, intimate and fervid love uniting the two, not in one flesh, but unfeignedly in one spirit."[84] In every instance, the basic reality, namely marriage, is always the same and Bernard uses it consistently throughout his sermons on the Song. In the first fourteen he is quite clear in the way he elaborates it. In the rest of the sermons, he only needs to allude to it since his readers are now well acquainted with it and know what he means.

The Uniqueness of Saint Bernard

As has already been mentioned, the nuptial allegory was developed by other authors before Saint Bernard, but they did so to a lesser extent or in a different manner. Saint Anselm, for example, just prior to him, ignored it entirely.[85] And one of Bernard's contemporaries, William of Saint-Thierry, seems to have been more reserved than was he: "William, unlike Bernard, does not identify married love as the figure of the highest affection, related most closely to the embrace of the soul and Christ her Bridegroom. He has little to say about human love in his *Exposition on the Song of Songs*."[86] Nevertheless, when speaking of the kiss, Bernard is precise, as has been shown in connection with those passages where the use of the Kiss symbolism is consciously grounded in the physiology of the real Kiss. In the next generation, Richard of Saint-Victor has still another approach when he speaks of the relationship uniting the Three Divine Persons.[87]

Gilbert of Hoyland, who continued Saint Bernard's *Sermons on the Song*, uses the marriage metaphor in an extremely realistic fashion. Commenting the verse of the *Song* "In my little bed by night, I sought him whom my soul loves" (3: 1), Gilbert writes: "Why does the bride say 'in my little bed' and not 'in a bed'? . . . Clearly in the diminutive I understand some restraint, so that the little bed is large enough for only the Beloved with the bride. For why not interpret restraint in a good sense, if a widening of the couch is turned into a reproach? 'You have spread wide your couch,' the Lord says through the prophet, 'you have welcomed an adulterer beside me' (Is. 57: 8) . . . . Rightly then the bride congratulates herself on her little bed. 'The couch is so narrow that one or other may fall out and the short blanket cannot cover both' (Is. 28: 5). *Both* means the husband and the adulterer."[88]

In transposing these images, Gilbert, unlike Bernard, does not work on the level of dogma or theology, but on that of the psychology of spiritual experience: he is speaking of the repose of the soul in contemplation. The author, who is considered to be the most "hesychastic" of Cistercian writers, frequently develops in this same vein the symbolism of the bed and the delights of the loving embrace.[89]

Further on in this text there is a hymn to disinterested love,[90] a hymn which is similar, but in no way equal, to those composed by Saint Bernard. At one point, it is true, we do find a clear distinction made between the espousals and marriage. The promise (*desponsatio*) is celebrated by a feast day, and it leads to "the bed and the vital warmth of affection." It is then that the nuptials (*nuptiae*) transform the fiancée into a bride. From this time on there can be no repudiation or divorce. The bridegroom must live ever after in his wife's house. The marriage is definitely sealed.[91] This is the time of the "use of love" (*usus amoris*) proper to married persons and during which they pay each other the marriage rights.[92] All this is illustrated by very forceful images, but they can hardly be translated.[93] These images are found in sermons which seem to have been written for nuns, and this confirms what has been written in another place concerning the absence of both repression and unhealthy complacency either in the author or in his lady audience and his male or female readers. Bernard and Gilbert write about the same facts and use the same language. But Gilbert is in no way Bernard's peer as a theologian and a poet. However, the observation remains: he uses the same allegory grounded in the same basic fact of life, namely, the love which normally exists between husband and wife.

There are some today who might wonder why these monks spoke so frankly and openly about conjugal love. Were they giving release to long-pent-up desires? We find nothing in their writings which is suggestive of either repression or obsession. And it is to be noticed that they mention these facts relatively little in comparison with all that they say on other subjects. Yet when they do mention them, they do not feel obliged to excuse themselves as if they had touched upon a taboo, a forbidden subject.[94] According to his own personality each one is either optimistic, idealizing to some extent lovemaking, or pessimistic, rejecting the facts for which he shows a certain contempt. It is the first of these two attitudes which is the more frequent, and it is found in the greatest of all these writers. There are still people who insist on repeating that because marriage has, necessarily, something to do with the flesh, it was held in little esteem in the twelfth century. But many texts prove the contrary: monastic authors must have considered marriage as being great and beautiful since they saw it as the symbol of the most sublime mysteries.

EIGHT

Harlot and Bride: Shadow Side and Coincidence of Opposites

❊

The Tradition of Prostitution as a Metaphor

Monks believed that there is such a thing as love in marriage, and consequently it was only normal that they should consider extramarital and loveless unions as something to be abhorred; and as for adultery, though it is to be reproved, it does not break the marriage bond and can even exist with love. Prostitution, however, is the antitype of marriage, its mere shadow. In the eyes of cloistral writers it is a negative element which led them to greater appreciation of the positive value of marriage. They reacted in many different and complex ways to prostitution, principally because it is something more than a social fact. Holy Scripture uses it quite frequently as a symbol of certain periods of crisis between God and his chosen People.[1] As such it has a positive value: it served as a metaphor just as did marriage. To have a clear grasp of the metaphorical signification of prostitution, we must start by recalling briefly the literary history of the theme and then go on to evoke the reality itself. We shall then be in a position to examine the different attitudes it called forth in Christians and especially religious writers.

So, in the biblical tradition, prostitution was both a social fact and a symbol. As a social reality, it was either profane or, in certain pagan religions, sacred. Nevertheless, it was constantly reproved by the writers of the Old and the New Testament. From time to time they invested it with a symbolical value, and it thus served as an image and a parable reminding the people of collective or individual infidelity to God or else summoning them to repentance and conversion. Examples of such infidelity are numerous: Delilah, who overcame Samson; the mother of Jephthah; Gomer, with whom the prophet Hosea united at the Lord's express command; the two harlots who squabbled over a baby in Solomon's presence; the great harlot mentioned in the Book of Revelation. These are all so many historical or symbolical images, and sometimes both at once. There are harlots mentioned in the genealogy of Christ, and they had a providential role in history. The Letter to the Hebrews[2] refering to Joshua,[3] praises those people who were saved by faith, and among them we find Rahab, of whom it is written: "By faith Rahab the harlot did not perish with those who were disobedient, because she had given friendly welcome to the spies." Commentators have put forth many a hypothesis in the attempt to explain the presence of this harlot among the cloud of witnesses.[4] And of course, we cannot forget Magdalen, whom Jesus defended and forgave. Each of the persons mentioned is written about in patristic and medieval literature, and it would be easy to quote many a passage proving this. The Bible itself, in the Book of Proverbs, gives a very pertinent description of the harlot who seeks to lure man into evil ways.[5] Is there any wonder that the paradoxical theme of the chaste harlot "should have become in patristic literature the symbol of the Church, who, though she is holy, is composed of sinners"?[6] In hagiography a well-known example is Saint Nicholas of Bari, who saved three young girls from prostitution. Legend and iconography transformed the girls into three children.[7]

In antiquity and throughout the Middle Ages the harlot was, according to a facile etymology, *meretrix a merendo mercedem*, a poor woman who earned her living as best she could by meriting her reward.[8] But she was also a professional who contrived by all possible means—dancing, singing, etc.—to set afire the imagination of men and to seduce married men, luring them away from their wives. Thus it was considered necessary to put people on their guard against men and women who were a menace to conjugal love: such were the courtesans, mimers, theater and ballet people, who displayed their bodies and their vices.[9] Some twenty to thirty categories were objects of general disapproval: all those who were known under the Latin equivalents of jesters, histrions, pantomimers, clowns, jongleurs, and so forth.[10] They were legion, and in the twelfth century Peter the Chanter remarked on the fact that when going abroad in public everyone came across harlots, jongleurs, and mimers.[11]

However, among all these people who were, juridically, infamous (*infames*), there were some men and women who had good sentiments, and all were open to some extent to conversion. In the eleventh century, when the clergy was so corrupt, the reformer monk Peter Damian found it necessary to denounce energetically, even violently, the danger of harlots. In the twelfth century it was stressed that these women were not altogether bad but only in their manner of life, and this they could abandon if they were only helped to do so. From the early beginnings of monastic literature we read famous examples of holy hermits who, at their own peril, sought out such women and brought them spiritual help. Converted harlots were known as "holy penitents": the records tell us of the niece of Saint Abraham, of Pelagia, and of Thaïs. The lives of such penitents were read over and over again, particularly the legends of Saint Mary the Egyptian and Thaïs. In the tenth century, for example, Hrotswitha wrote a drama based on the life of Thaïs; from the twelfth century onward this became a long novel in French.[12]

Prostitution as a Social Reality

During the period with which we are dealing, the interest in harlots was a manifestation of one of the many movements in favor of the poor which sprang up especially among hermits. These men not only practiced poverty but also witnessed to their predilection for the poor by preaching to the outcasts of society. Lepers and harlots flocked to hear hermit preachers announcing the good news of Christ, who loved Lazarus and forgave Mary Magdalen. The particular task of such preachers was to work for the rehabilitation in society of repentant women. Occasionally such action was a way of protesting against the hardly edifying behavior of certain unreformed cathedral chapters. Such an apostolate also met with great approval because poverty as an ideal was associated with that of purity. This was one of the consequences of the spiritual renewal which grew out of the Gregorian reform.[13]

In the twelfth century, Blessed Robert of Arbrissel founded at

Fontevrault a nunnery with four buildings. One was dedicated to Our Lady and was for virgins and widows; another, dedicated to Saint Benedict, was for the sick; a third was for lepers and placed under the patronage of Saint Lazarus; the fourth was dedicated to Magdalen and housed repentant harlots.[14] However, since not all these persevered in such a state of life, Vital of Savigny, also in the twelfth century, attempted to get them to marry lawful husbands.[15] These various initiatives paved the way for the reflections of canonists, theologians, and, consequently, the practical attitude of religious from the second half of the twelfth century onward.[16] The problem of prostitution was particularly debated at Paris, where so many clerics came to study. Different masters, Peter the Cantor, Robert of Courson, Stephen Langton, Peter of Poitiers, Martin, Thomas of Chobham, and others restated the two major traditional convictions but defined more clearly certain consequences and applications. They disapproved of prostitution, which meant that publicly known harlots who refused to repent were excommunicated: they were thus excluded from Mass and Holy Communion. If these punitive measures proved insufficient for the correction of such women, they could be driven out of the town. On the other hand, in spite of these severe measures, it was recommended that they be approached with a kindness and a charity inspired by compassion and the hope of bringing them to conversion. For this reason, they were allowed to come to church during prayers and were admitted to the kiss of peace. They were also allowed to offer candles at Sunday vespers with other women. And it was understood that they might keep the money which they had justifiably but illicitly earned. They had the right and even the duty to offer money for charitable causes. Such offerings were taken to be a sign of repentance and to show a desire for conversion. It was pointed out that Mary Magdalen anointed the Lord's feet with perfume bought with money earned by sinful ways. In particular, when Maurice of Sully was bishop at the time that Notre Dame was being built in Paris, harlots offered chalices and stained-glass windows. However, when this was known to the general public, it caused a certain amount of scandal, so theologians declared that such donations should only be accepted if they were made with fitting discretion. They argued that the fact of accepting such splendid gifts could be mistaken as a sign of approval of prostitution. So many different discussions help us to realize to what extent this social fact retained the attention of theologians and pastors. Fulkes of Neuilly, together with many other preachers, devoted much consideration to the subject. In their sermons they exhorted harlots to repent, and they did their best to help them to do so. Fulkes, for example, preaching in Paris in 1198, founded the Cistercian monastery of Saint Anthony on the outskirts of the town for repentant prostitutes who wished to live the monastic life. But he feared that not all such converts could persevere in continence. So he found another solution. Since, for reasons of poverty, many were unable to marry for want of a dowry and were thus practically forced into prostitution, he set up a fund destined to provide the necessary dowry. According to the chronicler Otto of Saint-Blasius, the students at Paris contributed 250 pounds of silver and the burghers more than 1,000 pounds. At the same time Innocent III declared that any man who saved a harlot from a brothel and married her would accomplish a work of mercy, acquiring merit for the remission of his own sins. This did not of course concern religious men: they had only an apostolic ministry. At Oxford, the regent of studies was charged with the catechesis of the students in connection with these women, for they were very numerous in the town.

From about 1140 onward, the monk Gratian fixed standards enabling future canonists to deal with prostitution as a whole.[17] They showed much comprehension for such cases but never gave way to sentiment, nor did they approve of the attitude of the harlots. They were, however, more understanding than Roman law: this was probably due to the influence of Christian charity. It was on the lines of such understanding that the teaching contained in the decretals developed. Furthermore, religious institutions were opened to receive former prostitutes as nuns. The aim was always conversion and the amendment of morals.[18]

Another echo of the attitudes towards prostitutes is found in the literature of the *miracula* and the *exempla*. The former were attributed to the saints and the latter were for the use of preachers, as we have already seen. These tables have, as we know, a common origin, even though they may have been composed in the late Middle Ages. The evil of prostitution is denounced, sometimes even by the Devil himself, who occasionally disguises himself as a harlot in order to tempt priests and faithful husbands. Women of evil lives were to be found in all walks of life, and one of them enslaved a king. Concubines of priests are assimilated to harlots. Sometimes, too, a woman and her complice are punished in the same way; for example, they die together being strangled by the same rope. We also read that a lion attacked a harlot and her *souteneur*. The Devil carries off their dead bodies. We also find mentioned rare exceptions of nuns who throw in their lot with such sinning women. But the more often it is these latter who are converted. Sometimes the Child Jesus turns his eyes away from them, or Christ enters into conversation with them. Men of God go and exhort them to mend their ways. They repent, confess their sins, and some retire into the desert.[19]

Gilbert of Nogent, Walter of Cluny, and William of Malmesbury describe the contrast existing between an abandoned wife and the sinner with whom her husband was living in adultery. The first is full of spite and arrogant in the manner she claims her rights, showing violence even in her prayer. The sinner on the contrary—the Latin word is the same as that used to describe Mary Magdalen—is humble and gentle: this is much more agreeable to the Virgin Mary. And we may suppose that the monks who recount this tale do so in order that it might serve as an example: humility and kindness are Christian and monastic virtues just as much as chastity is.[20] Among the Cistercians, Caesar of Heisterbach echos the "irresistible power of these women: there is nothing that they cannot get out of men." And he quotes the case of the guardian of the relics of Saint John the Baptist in the hospital dedicated to him at Jerusalem: "This shameless woman (*turpis femina*) corrupted him to the extent of getting him to sell to a merchant a whole arm of the Forerunner."[21] It is also true that the congenital frailty which is generally attributed to the female sex gives her right to special compassion: the monk and the novice whom Caesar portrays as dialoguing together agree that the priest is more at fault than his concubine.[22]

Sinner and Bride:
Mary Magdalen as a Model of Church Reform

The theme of the repentant harlot in love with Christ and become his bride was given a new dimension on account of a page of the Gospel and a happy historical error: The Gospel text in question is the moving pericope of Saint Luke, chapter 7, verses 36–50. We read there how

Jesus, a guest of the Pharisee Simon, is visited by a woman who is a notorious sinner in the town (*mulier quae erat in civitate peccatrix*).[23] She weeps and pours out perfume on the feet of the Lord. The Pharisee reproaches Jesus for allowing her to do this. But the Master defends her, forgives her, and praises her. She is not named, but Latin tradition, as a result of a confusion in texts and names, identifies her with Mary of Magdala, out of whom Jesus cast seven demons (Lk. 8: 2), and with Mary, the sister of Martha and Lazarus (Jn. 11: 4–43).[24] In this way, the sinner converted in the house of Simon became Mary Magdalen, and all that is said about the other two Marys is attributed to her. This is indeed a happy mistake! Or at least, so we are tempted to think! During the period of the first centuries of the Church, the repentant sinner was still considered to be a historical person: she gave Jesus the opportunity to say some daring things, but she was not proposed as a model to be imitated. However, with a little bit of invention and imagination, other details gradually were added to the facts stated in the Gospel. Mary Magdalen was said to have ended her days in Gaul living as a hermitess, and her relics were translated to Vézelay. Hagiographical and liturgical documents multiply in number, and at the same time her cult led to a more interiorized and deeper devotion: greater stress was laid on the effects of the workings of grace in her soul. Little by little people became more interested in the doctrinal aspect of her spiritual journey than in the facts of her life, thus she herself, as a person, became a focus of interest. Throughout the Latin Middle Ages, ingenious attempts were made to conjure up again all that she must have felt at the very instant of her conversion and also afterwards, in the various events of the lives of the other two Marys which were attributed to her. Thus grew up in the Church one of the most beautiful and richly significant legends.

This process of interiorization began with the splendid homily of Saint Gregory the Great on the encounter between the Risen Christ and Mary Magdalen on Easter morning.[25] This sermon contains the major themes: the force of love, the inner drama, the intensity of desire heightened by separation and the utter impossibility of physical contact, the wound of love, and other images borrowed from the Song of Songs. Saint Gregory mentions all this with great simplicity, almost with candor, without, however, departing from the elegant and formal beauty of expression which, by its lyricism, was an inspiration for love poets in the centuries which followed. This text, so beautiful among the beautiful, was read and reread publicly during divine office or privately in personal meditation. Certain Latin manuscripts give an abridged edition, omitting many of the more moving passages. This is the case, for example, of certain Carolingian homiliaries.[26] In the tenth century, Odo of Cluny wove this spiritual drama into the warp and weft of an account of the original gospel story, which, though still relatively brief, already contains the first threads of later embroiderings and a suggestion of Magdalen's feelings. One short sentence evokes her youthful years and then discreetly alludes to her inner state of soul: humility, repentance, love, desire of lasting union. At this stage in literary history, all this is supplied to the Church more than to individual souls. Magdalen is described as a new Eve because she symbolizes the rehabilitation of redeemed humanity and its readmission to the "familiarity" with God which had been lost by the sin of the first Adam.[27]

In the eleventh century there was a sort of Magdalenian ferment,[28] and this led to what might be styled a "Magdalen boom" in spiritual writings, particularly in hagiography but also—and this is less known—in the *preces,* formulas for private prayer. The legends and liturgical texts originated in and spread from a few important abbeys, especially Vézelay, Cluny, Fleury.[29] The movement spread from France to Italy and even to Rome under the patronage of Leo IX and other promoters of the Gregorian reform, with the result that the feast of Mary Magdalen was given increasing prominence in liturgical calendars. In the litanies she was given preeminence over other saints and was placed immediately after the Mother of God. The development of her cult was parallel with reforms in monasteries and in the Church as a whole—including the Church at Rome.[30] We may wonder why the image of Mary Magdalen was so in harmony with the movement for reform. The answer is to be found in the fact that this image corresponded to the two deepest convictions of the most fervent monastic milieux in those days. The first of these deeply rooted convictions is that we are all sinners both individually and collectively: as individuals we cannot fail to acknowledge our personal faults; as a social body, we acknowledge the secularization to which the Church has succumbed. In the second place, Mary Magdalen is an outstanding model of effective desire for conversion, return to God. She reminds us that personal conversion is possible for each one of us just as reform is possible for the Church. These are certainly monastic themes when we consider that monasticism is an institution favoring personal conversion and, by its example and influence, the reform of Church and society. Magdalen is a symbol of monastic love for God and other fellow beings: a humble, obscure, hidden love, a self-denying love, a contemplative love, an eminently faithful love. She who was once a harlot can become a bride for all eternity: a blessed bride of God (*O beata sponsa Dei*) as Saint Anselm exclaimed.[31]

It is this background of historical fact and intimate spiritual attitudes which led to the flashing outbreak of the Magdalenian image in the next age. Unceasingly throughout the twelfth century, stress was laid on the contrast between the greatness of her sin and the sincerity of her conversion. Raoul Ardent explains that in the Gospel Mary Magdalen is the sinner of sinners, the sinner par excellence. All other sinners mentioned in the New Testament are saints compared to her! The Lord expelled seven demons out of her—this means the greatest number possible—more than out of any other sinner. Her conversion was not the result of the preaching of one of the Apostles but a response to an inner call, "an intimate inspiration," and her penance was proportional to her sin. She loved because she was loved.[32]

Hugh of Saint-Victor goes further still and says that after conversion Mary Magdalen was totally pacified: she enjoyed a peace which she bought at great cost, absolute and lasting peace. The "mind's rest" which was hers in Christ allowed her to burn even more ardently with love.[33] All this is based on interiority. One of the many preachers of the period applied to her these words of Scripture: "Return to your heart"; and, again, these words handed down by tradition: "Know yourself." It was because Magdalen was so totally converted to God that she merited receiving the name of God's Mother, Mary. The two Marys are "stars," as is shown by the etymology of their name. However, Mary Magdalen is nearer to us because she has experience of temptation, sin, and inner warfare. This is why she is the model of both contemplative prayer and the prayer of intercession: she is a help to us in our tribulations.[34] The more we attempt to pierce her inner experience, the more she becomes a person for us: she ceases to be a model for the universal Church alone: she is also an example for every member of the Bride of Christ.

For the enlightenment of souls, preachers took inspiration from legend in order to describe the inner journey of Mary Magdalen. Honorius of Autun shows that her "worldly life" is the perfect antimodel of spiritual espousals with God. In her young days, she was married; then she ran away from her lawful husband and became a "vulgar harlot," living with "young lovers," "corrupt men," and "shameful lovers." But after a while she came back to her sister Martha's house and was there when Jesus came. After she had listened to him she became his disciple and spent in his service the money she had earned. Even after his death, she still had sufficient funds to embalm his body with costly ointments and spices. We notice that Mary Magdalen is attributed the actions of the three Gospel Marys as if she were the sole heroine of a single story. It is in this way that her evaluation from the lowest to the highest spiritual state is brought out. Her dignity is such that the Risen Christ appears to her before appearing to any of the apostles, and he even sends her on mission, making her the apostle of the apostles! It is not difficult to grasp why after the Lord's Ascension—as the legend holds—"on account of her love for him, she never wanted to see another man." She went off into the desert from whence she took her flight heavenwards. Indeed! this woman went through every stage leading from enslavement to the devil to "true freedom."[35]

Liturgical and literary texts applied many titles to Mary Magdalen, and it would be possible to compose a whole litany of such titles, all of which, in Latin, end with the suffix *ix*. We have, for example, *famulatrix Dei,* and two in particular sum up the whole of her mystery and her spiritual journey: she was *peccatrix* and *dilectrix,*[36] both sinner and lover. But while she was yet a sinner, she had already begun to be a lover, and when she attained the heights of "familiarity" with the Lord she remained conscious of her condition as a sinner. Abelard gives the meaning and the constant actuality of her message in two lines of verse:

> Peccatricis beatae solemnitas
> Peccatores maxime laetificat.[37]

Truly, indeed, we may agree with him, as did medieval authors, that "The solemnity of this blessed sinner greatly rejoices sinners." Mary

Magdalen is named a "blessed sinner" and even, according to some texts, "the most blessed of sinners" (*beatissima peccatrix*). As such she is a source of joy for all sinners. She is truly the most eminent of all sinners, be they men or women, who are mentioned in the Gospel. No one ever had as much contrition as she: she even became the mistress for all penitents who gave themselves up to the business of earning heavenly grace (*magistra omnium poenitentium in negotia caelestis gratiae acquirendae*).[38]

The Humble Sinner according to Saint Bernard

It will surprise no one that Saint Bernard added his note to this symphony of admiration. What, we may ask, was the particular contribution he made to this fashionable devotion about which so much had already been said by so many other writers? On this point, as on every other, he goes back to the sources. He makes no mention of the legend but comments the gospel story of Mary's conversion. Adopting the style of Scripture itself, he stressed the contrast which Jesus remarked upon between the Pharisee who thought himself to be just and the woman who was only too conscious that she was a sinner. The whole of the Abbot of Clairvaux's teaching on humility and love is compacted into the few passages devoted to Magdalen. The Song of Songs provided a very suitable background, allowing Bernard to situate the mystery of Mary Magdalen in the context of the bridal union between Christ and his Church. The Bridegroom and the Bride delight in mutual embrace in those members of the Church who have already entered into eternal glory. Those who are still waiting expectantly in hope are like those virgins attendant on the bride and waiting patiently outside the nuptial chamber. Such are the souls who have never been sullied in worldly embracings and also the repentant harlots who once gave themselves up to shameful prostitution, dragged down as they were by every fleshly desire. These latter are all the more ardent to reform their ways in that they set about the work of repentance so much later than the others. Mary Magdalen is a comforting example, a model of conversion from savage, uncontrolled love to faithful bridal love. "Penitents rejoice! And you who are still weak, take comfort!"[39] In the vocabulary of tradition and Saint Bernard, the "penitents" are first of all monks, among whom are some feeble souls (*pusillanimes*) more recently converted to monastic life.

The repentant sinner of the Gospel went through all the states of soul which these new recruits feel: the memory of sin, the marks it leaves, their confusion, and even sometimes the trouble they feel. All this Magdalen felt when she poured out her spikenard on the Lord's feet.[40]

Bernard reconstructed Magdalen's experience on the basis of his own and that of his monks, which was well known to him: "She still felt the stirrings of her former passions which had not yet died out in her."[41] But she fled to prayer and trusted in the benefits God accorded to all mankind. This afforded her some measure of consolation. And though she was still a sinner and known as such in the town, she was moved with great love, and this led to her being preferred to Simon the Pharisee, who judged only by appearances.[42] Jesus could read hearts and he knew that Magdalen was already a more "accomplished person"[43] than Simon. It is always this contrast between the two which repeatedly occurs as a sort of leitmotiv, even after the Resurrection, "when she was no longer a sinner as the Pharisee reproached her."[44] Magdalen was "made righteous" just as were the humble publican, the adulterer David, Paul the persecutor. The Pharisee did not know that justification, i.e., holiness, is a gift from God and not the fruit of human labor; when the Lord no longer imputes iniquity to a person, then this person is not only righteous but also blessed. The Pharisee imagines that he has no need of forgiveness. "But the Lord, that most Righteous Man, once he was touched by a sinful woman, imparts to her something of his own righteousness, without losing any himself. . . ." Bernard illustrates further on in his sermon the coexistence of sinfulness and righteousness stemming from forgiveness when he mentions the theme of the bride who is black but beautiful. She who was once a harlot is now a bride.[45]

On more than one occasion, Bernard took a certain delight in contrasting, more or less profusely, loving humility and self-sufficient pride, symbolized by Magdalen and by the Pharisee. All the "pious" people—Simon, Martha, Peter, and the other disciples—were against Magdalen, but Jesus gave her the privilege, the prerogative of his preferential love when he became her advocate,[46] her defense. It is not the pious, but the sinner who shows God's willingness to forgive mankind. Magdalen, a most notorious sinner, received an abundant grace of love from the first instant of her conversion, and afterwards she was admitted to divine familiarity. The Pharisee murmured and criticized; all the other witnesses accused her; Jesus alone excused and forgave her. And it is this divine liberality of forgiveness which wins her the unique privilege, the unheard of preference by which she was allowed to touch his feet and be the first to see him after his Resurrection.[47] When she entered the house of Simon she had already ceased to be a sinner. Her way of behaving with Jesus showed that she had already repented of her sins and that she had become loving, gentle, humble, full of the spirit of the beatitudes." "That is why, O you Pharisee, she is no longer to be called a sinner, as your sentence would have it, but holy, a disciple of Christ."[48]

In all these texts which overflow with love for Christ and for Magdalen, she is never called by any other name than that of the "sinner," though certain texts written at Fleury call her *meretrix*,[49] and some preachers persist in mentioning that she "gave herself to prostitution in public for a low price."[50] In spite of this, Bernard gives her the title she has in the Gospel: this is her dignity and her right to glory. *Meretrix* is nothing more than the name of a profession, and it sets Magdalen in a socially humilitating category, whereas the title *sinner* is a theological point of view and places her in a spiritual category: a class of people for whom Jesus shows preferential love and whom he admits to his familiarity. There are men and women in this category: they have in common that they know themselves to be sinners and that they are loved, even so, by Jesus, who forgives and saves them. And they pay him love for love.

Sinner and Lover: in the Wake of Saint Bernard

It seems that all the writers who came after Saint Bernard and followed in his wake had nothing further to add, almost as though he had said all there was to say. We do find some interesting texts, and some are quite beautiful, but they are hardly more than variations on the Bernardine themes, developments and occasionally facile elaborations of ideas he had hinted at. No one ever came up to his standard. Nicholas of Clairvaux develops a little the contrast between the Pharisee and Magdalen: this is the symbol of the immense abyss separating not only pride from humility, but also the strict observance of legal niceties from the freedom which blooms in love.[51] Nicholas also states quite clearly that because of Magdalen's burning love for Christ the King, he became all in all to her: the beloved, the lover, love itself, and even, this is the last word, "her bridegroom."[52]

Gilbert of Hoyland, who continued Bernard's sermons on the Song of Songs, took up again the traditional symbols but used them more strongly, possibly more clumsily than had done his master, Bernard. For example, he stresses the difference between the stench caused by Mary Magdalen's sins and the sweet perfume of the ointment she poured out on the Lord's feet and her reputation after this loving gesture. The grace of forgiveness is never delayed: in the course of the meal in Simon's house she was immediately forgiven and loved in preference to the Pharisee.[53] In the *Short Commentary on the Song of Songs,* which seems to have been principally the work of William of Saint-Thierry, we read that her perfume rejoiced even the angels.[54] Here again, in this text as in all the others, she is named the sinner. There was, however, something different about her which distinguished her from other sinners: her love had a special quality about it. Among all those who loved Christ, "Peter was ardent, John gentle, but the sinner was humble."[55] *Peccatrix humilis:* that is the title she receives in the litany of the holy people in the Gospel.

Armand of Bonneval, who continued the *First Life* of Saint Bernard after the death of William of Saint-Thierry, evokes Magdalen's friendship for Jesus in exact and beautiful words. He recalls the kisses bestowed on the Lord's feet, the ointment which was poured out with a lavishness contrasting with the avarice of Judas, and Magdalen's fidelity to Jesus not only during his life, but also after his death: "Since she had no man with whom to live, she spent all her zeal on this one dead Man."[56] Peter of Celle, another of Bernard's contemporaries who corresponded with him and read his works, devotes no less than five sermons to Mary Magdalen.[57] With his customary poetic verve he exalts all that distinguishes Magdalen from the Pharisee: faith in Jesus, trust in prayer, generosity in sacrificing all she possessed. She and Mary the Mother of Jesus received different gifts from the same Holy Spirit of God. And, like the prodigal son, Magdalen "came back to herself"; she came back to her heart, and the author describes for us the dialogue which went on within her and led her to make the decision to come back to the Lord. When she kisses his feet, it is with sentiments of great humility. Peter of Celle imagines what she must have felt at that moment of grace and says that her inner dispositions then give weight to her present intercession for us. He goes on to say, may she pray for us, "This most holy sinner, this beloved one of Jesus who never hesitated in her love for him." Truly, Magdalen is now a mediatrix between the Lord and us. She meditates aloud in our presence and speaks of him whom her soul loves. She tells us why she came to him. The seven demons had despoiled her of any moral worth, and at this point Peter of Celle describes realistically the various articles of clothing and the ornaments which were taken away from her like so many lost virtues.[58] The symbolism of spiritual nakedness is followed by that of the bed, rest, and sleep. Magdalen was indeed instantly clothed with unparalleled beauty. Every detail helps us to follow her in her spiritual journey until she meets with the Risen Christ, he who "brought a sick person back to health, made a leper clean, turned a sinner into a saint and a harlot into an apostle."[59] All this is sketched against the background of the pride and stubborn-heartedness of the Pharisee, and this sheds even more light on the repentance, the tears, and the love of the sinful woman.

Aelred of Rievaulx, disciple and admirer of Saint Bernard, takes us one step further along the path of interiority. His text is shorter and more sober than Peter's but goes to the heart of the life of prayer. Writing for his sister recluse, the abbot of Rievaulx advises her to identify with Mary Magdalen and to go on loving in silence and apparent separation. He writes:

> Enter now into the house of the Pharisee and gaze upon your Lord reclining there. With that most blessed sinner draw near to his feet. Wash them with tears, wipe them with your hair, cover them with kisses, and anoint them with ointment. If up to now he has refused to allow you to approach his feet, insist, pray, raise up your eyes swollen with tears and with deep and unutterable groanings, drag out of him what you are asking for. Combat with God as did Jacob so that he may rejoice in being overcome. It will seem that he turns his eyes away from you sometimes, that he turns a deaf ear, that he hides the feet you so desire. Nevertheless insist in season and out of season; cry out to him "How long wilt thou hide thy face from me? How long shall I cry out without being heard? Restore to me the joy of thy salvation, O good Jesus because my heart says to thee, Thy face O Lord do I seek, thy face alone." And surely he will not refuse a virgin those feet which he allowed a sinner to kiss.[60]

Thus, throughout Saint Bernard's century the ideas which were scattered here and there in his own writings and his daily monastic teaching recurred in texts which explore the themes he had suggested and go more deeply into them. Stephen of Tournai commanded a regular canon to "imitate Magdalen the sinner. She wept over herself, over her brother, and over the Lord." Magdalen's tears are the symbol of all the activities of the contemplative life and of every form of Christian fellowship in solidarity.[61] Soon after this period, Caesar of Heisterbach collated the marvelous memories of the first Cistercian century, and it was then that were related the two "miracles" in which Mary Magdalen appeared to a sick monk during the night and healed him[62] and helped another to cross a river so that he could go and celebrate Mass.[63] Other exempla are also recalled: her conversion, her long life of penitence with which she ended her earthly days; her apparition, in the form of a beautiful woman, to a cleric living in sin who repented in imitation of her. Another of these edifying tales tells how a virgin who boasted that she was better than Mary Magdalen fell into sinful ways so that she might learn the necessary lesson of humility.[64] A similar lesson of humility is given, though in a different way, to a Cistercian in a tale related by Conrad of Eberbach: "To another devout and religious brother, it was given to see in the spirit blessed Mary Magdalen standing before the altar with shining face and raiment. When he saw her the brother was filled with great joy. And while he was meditating with wishful and beseeching mind and sighing with the fervor of a great holy desire to see the Blessed Virgin Mary, Mother of God, whom he most devoutly served day and night, he heard a voice coming to him in the vision which said: 'It behooves you to know that you are not yet worthy to look upon the most sublime brightness of the immaculate and virginal Mother of God. Do your best then, grow and progress as much as you are able so that you may merit seeing her.' "[65]

As we can notice, all these tales gradually introduce the marvelous, whereas earlier spiritual writers confined themselves to gospel facts even though they occasionally added more or less elaborate theological considerations. This is to be explained by the fact that during the second half of the twelfth century the "Claravallian" school, and probably Clairvaux itself, at least those authors who were acquainted with Saint Bernard's writings, produced the longest text that had so far been written about Mary Magdalen: *The Life of Saint Mary Magdalen and Saint Martha*. This *Life*, which was long attributed to

Rhaban Maur,[66] closes the cycle begun with Odo of Cluny and is a very subtle combination of two different sets of fact. It weaves together the basic elements found in Odo's sermon and the psychological and theological developments penned by Bernard. The literary embellishments are quite in harmony with the style of courtly romances. Such embellishments include the descriptions of Magdalen's worldly, physical beauty, the adventures she lived during her spiritual journey, the description of which is based on Bernard's theory of self-knowledge. Three major events are stressed: she sins, she repents, she is defended by Jesus.

The narration contains the different Gospel scenes depicting the forgiveness accorded to Mary, the raising of Lazarus, her brother, from the dead, which is also a symbol of forgiveness. Mary is described preparing the spikenard which she is going to offer to her "friend" and details are given of the caresses and kisses she lavishes on the Lord's feet. Then we have the description of Mary listening to him, contemplating him, accepting to be separated from him and remaining faithful to him in the suffering of separation, for she knows that later on, in eternity, she will be allowed to embrace him. She did not suffer what other lovers suffer when they are separated, because she did not lose her Lover: he merely left before her (*cum nec amiserit amotorem, sed praemiserit*).[67] She sighs and longs for him, hungering and thirsting to see the face of her beloved until, "in the wedding bed of eternal contemplation, she throws herself round his neck with most gentle and sweet embracings."[68] And indeed, when she is about to breathe her last, she hears a voice calling her in the words of Psalm 44: "Come, my loved one . . . the most beautiful among the children of men desires your beauty. . . ."[69] The whole story is spangled with quotations from the Song of Songs and the doctrinal commentaries which Saint Bernard made on them. Here too, as in the tradition of Vézelay, there are many feminine words but she is also *dilectrix, contemplatrix, ministratrix, amatrix* because she was also *primo peccatrix*, first of all a sinner[70] and then, for all eternity, united to him in "intimate love."[71] "O blessed sinner, O most ardent lover, blessed is the soul who is with you!"[72] One could hardly wish for a more complete synthesis of all monastic devotion to Mary Magdalen than this Cistercian and Claravallian reinterpretation of a Cluniac source.

To have love for the sinful woman because she loved him alone who can forgive us: seen from this point of view, the theme ceases to be the particular sin of prostitution and opens out to include the whole mystery of sin and forgiveness. The antimodel of holiness is not luxury, but pride. The model is no longer drawn from the Old Testament, but from the new covenant of love in the Gospel.

Thus, for prostitution, as for conjugal love, the metaphor is always founded on a basic reality: the antimodel exists: it is to be observed and judged. The negative aspects are to be reproved, they are breaches of marriage and of true love. But this antimodel also has its positive aspects: it is always to be hoped that the situation is not irremediable. The presupposed and proposed model is conjugal love. However, the very fact of the existence of other types of union between a man and a woman leads us to see that conjugal love is the normal form and that it has peculiar and inherent difficulties, temptations, and weaknesses: these too are to be observed and judged, with compassion. They are foreseen and, if possible, forestalled. Should it be too late, then every effort is to be made to bring the situation back to normal.

This fundamental fact had always been traditionally interpreted in the light of Scripture as well as in the light of patristic and monastic literature. And this is true of the twelfth century as in the preceding ones. The novelty lay in the field of canon law and spirituality. Spiritual literature acquired certain more delicate and psychological nuances as well as deeper theological considerations. And it was expressed in more realistic, vivid, poetical, or suggestive terms. The evolution was a move forward: the impetus came mainly from Saint Bernard, with his keen perception of the Christian experience and his talent as a writer. Throughout this period we assist at a transition from the simple observation of a social fact and a rigid moral judgment to the analysis of inner sentiments. The statement of objective, universal, and ecclesial values is allied with a more careful consideration of subjective, personal, interior aspects.

This led to a more penetrating insight of the two complementary aspects of what certain psychologists call the "archetype" of the prostitute who is submitted to the demands of an outer, physical activity and yet sufficiently free to assert herself by rising above such a condition.[73] In biblical words, this is the projection of the antagonism existing between the law and love, symbolized by the Pharisee and the harlot. She was able to love and be loved and thus to become, in her own way, a bride in her relations with God and man. This antagonism and its solution—the preference given to love rather than to the strict observance of moral principles—was formulated in the Gospel in connection with Hosea.[74] It took tradition into consideration. But it was especially during the twelfth century that it became clear. And this because of a woman who evoked a reminiscence of the Old Testament, one who was also an illustrious example, the perfect Christian illustration of the archetypal harlot: Mary Magdalen.

Epilogue

A question we may ask at the close of this study is whether the Christian Middle Ages were truly ignorant of desire and tenderness and considered love an affair for extramarital relations, as is still being said.[1] And we even find that C.S. Lewis and D. de Rougemont are still being quoted as authorities on the matter.[2] Yet, in 1975, Henry Ansgar Kelly showed the "unhistorical" nature of the theory according to which love between man and woman is to be found only in courtly love, considered as love in adultery.[3] The author, in his very well-informed book, destroyed such a construction. His sources were mainly Chaucer and his times, but he also went back to the sources of Chaucer and showed that Ovid was "the West's first champion of conjugal love."[4] Among the canonists and theologians, Kelly studied mainly the opinions of the end of the twelfth century and the thirteenth century,[5] but he was careful to point out that thirteenth-century theologians tended to be more severe than the spiritual writers of the twelfth century. He quoted in particular Hugh of Saint-Victor.[6] Thus we may say that historians acknowledge that love in marriage was a real thing.

While the pages of this book were being written, the documentation concerning the subjects touched upon here proliferated, and for that reason it seems useful to conclude with a few complementary facts confirming the results exposed in this work.

Different documents, in particular funereal inscriptions, show that conjugal love existed in ancient Greece and Rome.[7] However, it is to be noted that such inscriptions were more numerous and more explicit in Christian Rome. This is shown in a study in archeology which, it is to be hoped, will be published. Among the "human relations" witnessed to by the epitaphs, there are several dozen instances of love between husband and wife. They do not mention merely fidelity: this could well be something purely juridical. But we also find sweetness and tenderness listed as elements in conjugal love. Often enough, as is only natural, such declarations of love are expressed poetically in love songs (carmina) which extol the joys of love.[8] This is quite in harmony with what we established on the basis of patristic texts.[9]

For the long series of centuries which are called the Middle Ages, the few documents previous to the twelfth century which have been mentioned here seem to show that, in those days too, married Christians lived in love and knew the pleasures of love without feeling guilty. However, as social structures advanced, they raised new problems, mainly of the juridical order of things. During the twelfth century and afterwards, such problems were more clearly formulated. Solutions were provided when individual cases were submitted to papal judgment,[10] and especially with the development of ecclesiastical[11] and secular institutions.[12]

In the field of noninstitutional literature, themes were frequently borrowed from the "garden of love" mentioned by the Song of Songs.[13] Furthermore, a growing number of monks and nuns, originating from knightly circles,[14] had been sensitized to the realities of human love and some even had experience of it.[15] The expositions of the Song of Songs which Saint Bernard made to his monks were translated into the vernacular.[16] The Jewish community of Troyes, was not far from the places where Bernard of Clairvaux and Chrétien de Troyes, to mention but two names in particular, had frequent contacts with Jewish communities of other regions, especially in Spain and in Provence.[17] The literary and religious images and ideas freely circulated among these different groups. The legacy of ancient Greece and Rome continued to be a source of inspiration.[18] The Crusades and other reasons for separation made "love from afar" a reality for many a married couple.[19] A monastic and probably Cistercian source influenced, directly or indirectly, the Quest of the Grail.[20] In many different ways the love lyric was "redeemed."[21]

It is not at all astonishing that the greatest singer of love in the twelfth century, Saint Bernard of Clairvaux, should have had a lasting influence on poets and theologians who were as realistic and as profound as he. And this, not only during his own century[22] but in the following centuries also. For example, when Saint Francis de Sales applied the metaphor of the kiss to God, more than once he made express mention of Saint Bernard's teaching. But he summarized and translated it into his own charming language. The union of the Word and human nature in the Incarnation is described as "this mystery in which Wisdom proceeding from the mouth of the Most High unites to our flesh."[23] The theme is taken up again and developed, in connection with the answer Mary gave at the Annunciation: "Let this Word, which is the word of the Father, proceeding from his mouth, come and unite to me by the medium of the Holy Spirit he who is the eternal sigh of love of the Father to his Son and reciprocally of the Son to his Father."[24] Here again, the basic reality of the metaphor is previously exposed and even described with precision, as may be seen by the following words: "Now, making the Bride speak first, as though in a certain surprise of love, he makes her first utter this exclamation: '*Let him kiss me with the kiss of his mouth!*'. . . From all time the kiss, as by natural instinct, has been used to represent perfect love, that is, union of hearts, and not without cause . . . . In this way, when we kiss each other, we apply one mouth to the other, to show that we would pour out our souls, reciprocally, the one to the other, and thus unite them in perfect union. For this reason, in all ages and among the holiest men in the world, the kiss is the sign of love and consent."[25]

Texts of both the Old and the New Testament illustrate at length this truth: "When the divine Spirit wishes to express perfect love, he almost always uses words of union and conjunction . . . . Love is unique, unifying, drawing, binding, gathering together all things and bringing them to unity . . . . Thus the end of love is nothing other than the union of the lover and the thing loved."[26]

This sort of analogy, applied to the Trinity, is not found in the works of Abelard, who gave his explanations in more abstract categories.[27] But when he allowed the poet in him to write, and in particular in his *Hymnary,* the language of love came into its own again.[28] And it is even thought that in his hymn to Mary Magdalen there is a delicate and discreet allusion to Héloïse, echoed even more discreetly by Peter the Venerable.[29]

Moreover, we may ask whether the letters exchanged between Abelard and Héloïse after their marriage and then after their separation could have come into being without a certain context. For Héloïse the background was formed by the Abbey of Argenteuil, where she was a nun after having been first a pupil; and for Abelard, the context was the Cloister of Notre Dame, the schools where he taught, the monasteries where he lived. In all these places the literature of human love was not only impregnated with the sense of the presence of God but also permeated with the love experiences of the surrounding society. The adolescent Héloïse, an orphan, is supposed to have said—and there is some possibility that this is so—that when her companions went out and met their families, they were "informed" with regard to sexual matters as to their thoughts and ways of doing.[30] When they went out walking together in the monastery grounds, and later near the Cloister of Notre Dame, they surely chatted about the dreams of every young girl. The lovers were persons out of the ordinary: Héloïse because she was the niece of a canon who was perhaps a jealous priest and lived an almost monachal existence in his house; Abelard because he was a professor of genius in whom success raised passions and problems. Their extramarital love, though it was exceptional, was in many respects normal, and entailed procreation. This, then, was not reserved to marriage. After their marriage, their lawful separation by mutual consent was one more example of frequent practice. The favor they enjoyed from the great of this world who helped them to found the Paraclete, make it prosper and have recruits; the spiritual help given to Héloïse by Saint Bernard, Peter the Venerable, Innocent II; all this goes to show that not only were they not misunderstood by the society of their times, but that, far from being ostracized, they were helped. Abelard's doctrinal difficulties were of another order of things. But their love affair and its different vicissitudes was in keeping with what society was then able to understand, even though it was neither commonplace nor ordinary. The only extraordinary thing about all this was the spiritual quality, the psychological insight, and the literary talent with which such sentiments of human love between Christians was expressed.

As to Andrew the Chaplain, who also wrote on love, the most recent works insist on the refinement of his erotic language[31] and confirm the true nature of his writing on love, which is nothing less than a *Contra amorem*.[32] His "wiles" and his "industrious dialectics,"[33] in which there is "more humor than malice," explain his success with the Parisian students of the second half of the thirteenth century, "clerics whose most daring flirts he probably inspired. It is certain, in fact, that the profound moral and disciplinary disorders went hand in hand with doctrinal troubles."[34]

This had not been so during the twelfth century—at least according to the picture sketched by the monastic writers who have been brought together here. Doubtless, this image is incomplete. But it is one which must be taken into account if we wish to acquire a comprehensive knowledge of this period which has its own particular charm.

The opening lines of Alan of Lille's long hymn extolling marriage will serve as a fitting conclusion:

> O how great is the dignity of marriage which began in Paradise and removes the vice of incontinence, containing in itself a heavenly sacrament. Marriage which preserves the faith of the marriage bed, maintaining between the partners a single society of life, and frees progeny from shame, excusing fleshly intercourse from fault. In this state the patriarchs were saved, and in this same state certain of the Apostles were chosen. O what great strength is in this sacrament: lest any man should fall into the precipice of luxury or incontinence, he is sustained by honest union.[35]

Notes

✣

Introduction

1. To the bibliography given by M. Sheehan, "Choice of Marriage Partner in the Middle Ages: Development and Mode of Application of a Theory of Marriage," in *Studies in Medieval and Renaissance History*, vol. 1 (The University of British Columbia, 1978), pp. 3-4, add *Famille et sexualité dans l'Occident médiéval*, ed. G. Duby and J. Le Goff (Paris 1977).

2. All these points have been the object of fruitful studies on the part of M. Sheehan. The results have been summarized in the study cited in the preceding note. I thank him for having encouraged me to approach these problems.

3. G. Duby, *Medieval Marriage. Two Models from Twelfth-Century France* (Baltimore and London: John Hopkins University Press, 1978). On the consequences which the fact of belonging to the nobility could have on the attitudes to marriage and celibacy, see A. Murray, *Reason and Society in the Middle Ages,* (Oxford 1978), pp. 342-49, 369-73 and passim.

4. Part of the documentation used in the following pages was the subject matter of two papers: "Love in Marriage in Twelfth-Century Europe" (University of Tasmania, Occasional Paper 13, 1979); "L'amour dans le mariage vu par des religieux," (Paper read at the Catholic University of Louvain in 1978). In the pages to come, any title which is not preceded by the name of an author is a publication in which I have dealt at greater length on subjects which can only be briefly mentioned here.

Chapter 1

1. J. T. Noonan, Jr., "Marital Affection in the Canonists," in *Studia Gratiana XII, Collectanea Stephan Kuttner,* ed. J. Forchielli and A. M. Stickler, 2 (Bologna 1967): 479-510.

2. G. Le Bras, "Mariage," in *Dictionnaire de théologie catholique, IX, 2* (Paris 1927), col. 2134-36.

3. J. A. Brundage, "Concubinage and Marriage in Medieval Canon Law," in *Journal of Medieval History* 1 (1975): 1-17.

4. For Roman law, for example see: *Ulp., Dig.*, 21, 1, 32, 13: *Non enim coitus matrimonium facit, sed affectio maritalis;* for late and patristic Latinity, see texts in *Thes. Ling. lat.*, vol. 1, (Leipzig 1900, 1911); vol. 4, (1906–9), p. 322; ancient Christian inscriptions are reproduced by H. Leclercq, "Mariage," in *DACL,* vol. 10, part 2 (Paris 1932), cols. 1953–59; in *Reallexikon für Antike und Christentum,* art. "Ehe," vol. 4, col. 662–99. A particularly dense text is found in *l'Historia Apollonii Regis Tyri,* which will be cited below. For the Middle Ages, to the texts cited by Noonan, "Marital Affection," add, for example Rathier of Verona (Xe.s.), *dilectio maritalis,* in *Praeloquia,* III, *PL* 136, 242.

5. Guntharius Archiep. Coloniensis (d. 873), "Diabolica ad Nicolaum papam," in *MGH., Scriptores rer. germ.* 1886, pp. 68–70. We could well apply to the Middle Ages what has been written about the seventeenth and eighteenth centuries: "If inclination is not obligatory, and if in most cases, it is not the major reason for the choice of partners, then that does not mean that it does not develop later. Love in marriage has this in particular about it, that it truly starts *after marriage* and is furthered by cohabitation. It does not push two separated people together, it pushes two beings who live together to please each other and to become attached to one another," P. Aries, "L'amour dans le mariage et en dehors," in *La Maison-Dieu* 127 (1976): 140.

6. J. T. Noonan, Jr., "Power to Choose," in *Viator* 6 (1973): 410–34. The care to guarantee the freedom to marry and to choose one's partner was such that, from the time of Gratian onward, a raped girl could marry the man if she found that a way to free herself from the pressure of parents: J. A. Brundage, *Rape and Marriage in Medieval Canon Law,* in *Revue de droit canonique* 28 (1978): 74–75.

7. Noonan, "Marital Affection", pp. 497–502.

8. Ibid., pp. 502–9.

9. References to the words cited here are to be found in *Thes. ling. lat.,* vol. 1 (Leipzig, 1900), col. 1206–12; *Mittellateinisches Wörterbuch,* vol. 1 (Munich 1967), col. 353–54.

10. Texts are quoted in the article "Cor et cordis affectus" in *Dictionnaire de spiritualité,* vol. 2 (1953), col. 2278–2300.

11. Texts in J. Châtillon, "Devotio," in *Dictionnaire de spiritualité,* vol. 3 (1957), col. 702–16.

12. *Affectualis, affectualitas, affectualiter* are read in Gilbert of Nogent and elsewhere. In William of Saint-Thierry, and other authors, *affectus* has the strong sense of "self-donation" (Hingabe) as has been shown by W. Zwingmann, "Ex affectu mentis: Über die Vollkommenheit menschliche Handelns und menschlicher Hingabe nach Wilhelm von Saint Thierry," in *Cîteaux: Commentarii Cistercienses* 18 (1967): 5–37, and "Affectus illuminare amoris. Über das Offenbarwerden der Gnade und Erfahrung von Gottes beseligender Gegenwart," ibid. 18 (1967): 193–226.

13. *Sup. Cant.,* 49, 5–50, *S. Bernardi opera,* 2 (Rome 1958), 2: 75–83.

14. *De diligendo Deo,* 27–28, *S. Bernardi opera,* 3 (Rome 1963), 3: 142–43.

15. *De diversis*, 50, 2–3, *S. Bernardi opera*, vol. 6, part 1 (Rome 1970), pp. 271–72.

16. *Diplomata Karoli III, M.G., Dipl. reg. Germ. Karol.*, 2 (1936–37): 7, date: 878.

17. *Diplomata Conradi II, M.G., Dipl. reg. et imp. Germ.*, vol. 4 (1909), no. 112, p. 156, l. 22, date: mid-eleventh century.

18. "Dulcissima coniux" or "uxor," "amantissima coniux" or "uxor": frequent and sometimes united formulas: "tibi dulcissime atque amantissime uxori meae" (ed., L. Serrano, *Cartulario de San Vicente de Oviedo* [Madrid 1929], p. 512, date: 1179). Only a few characteristic formulas can be cited here. Mrs. A. M. and Mr. R. H. Bautier were kind enough to help me in my research in the diplomatic field. I thank them.

19. "Dilecta et amabilis coniu(x) mea," (E. Falaschi, ed., *Carte dell' Archivio capitolare di Pisa*, vol. 1 [930–1050], [Rome 1971], p. 126, date: 1015), same formula further on, p. 127.

20. "Sub interventu nostre dilecte coniugalis Gisle", *Dipl. Conr. II, ed. cit.*, p. 145, date: 1030. *Dipl. Heinrici II, M.G. Dipl. reg. et imp. Germ.* vol. 3, p. 534; mid-eleventh century.

21. "Haec autem coniunctio amoris et divisio honoris facta est coram domno Petro rege", (J. M. Lacarra, ed., *Coleccion diplomatica de Irache*, vol. 1 [958–1222], [Saragossa 1965], p. 106, date: 1103).

22. "Adamavi te, o dulcissima sponsa . . . et a parentibus et propinquis tuis exquisivi te . . ." (M. Fauroux, ed., *Recueil des actes des ducs de Normandie (911–1066)*, [Caen 1961], p. 84, date 996–1008).

23. "Ut te in coniugio copularem sociam . . . . Obinde propter amorem, honorem dulcedinis tuae et pro coniugalis gratiam et pro federe conligando dono . . . in hunc dotis titulum . . .", (L. Serrano, ed., *Cartulario de monasterio de Vega con documentos de San Pelavo Vega de Oviedo* [Madrid 1927], p. 25, date: 1075).

24. E. Casanova, ed., *11 Cartulario della Berardenga*, vol. 1 (Sienna, 1927), p. 536, date: 1140.

25. "Propter spaeciem et pulchritudinem tuam do et dono tibi . . ." (S. Garcia Larragueta, ed., *Colección de documentos de la Catedral de Oviedo* [Oviedo 1962], p. 245, date: 1081).

26. "Uxorem dilectam . . ." (Thietmar de Mersebourg, *Chronicon, M.G., Script. rer. Germ.*, vol. 9, p. 6, 34–35, date: 1012–18).

27. P. Rousset, "La femme et la famille dans l' 'Histoire ecclésiastique' d'Orderic Vital," in *Zeitschrift für Schweizerische Kirchengeschichte* 63 (1969): 58–66.

28. J. Frappier, *La poésie lyrique française aux XIIe et XIIIe siècles. Les auteurs et les genres* (Paris 1966), p. 79.

29. P. Bec, ed., *La lyrique française du Moyen-âge. (XIIe–XIIIe siècles)*, vol. 2, Textes (Paris 1978), pp. 92–94. Other examples of Crusade chansons ibid., pp. 85–99. The same author studies this literary genre ibid., vol. 1 Etudes (Paris 1977), pp. 150–58. On the evolution of the genre, see J. C. Payen, " 'Peregris': De l' 'amor de longh' au congé courtois. Notes sur l'espace

et le temps de la chanson de croisade," in *Cahiers de civilisation médiévale* 17 (1974): 247-55.

30. Text in *Historiens occidentaux des croisades* vol. 3, pp. 887-90; on the circumstances in which these letters were written, see H. Hagenmeyer, *Chronologie de la première croisade* (Paris, 1902), pp. 140-41.

31. Texts have been quoted in this sense, by P. Scheuten, *Das Mönchtum in der altfranzösischen Profandichtung (12-14. Jahrhundert)* (Münster 1919), pp. 26-29.

32. Ilene Forsyth, "The Theme of Cockfighting in Burgundian Romanesque Sculpture", in *Speculum* 53 (1978): 264-65.

33. Bernold de Constance, *Chronicon, M.G.S.S.*, V. pp. 392.

34. H. E. von Kausler, ed., . . ., *Würtembergisches Urkundenbuch,* I, I-VIII, Stuttgart, 1849-1903, t. V, app. 7, p. 374, date 1100.

35. Conradus Saxo, *Speculum beatae Mariae Virginis,* 15, ed. (Quaracchi 1904), p. 225, 13th century.

36. Dan. 13.

37. H. Taviani, "Le mariage dans l'hérésie de l'an mil," in *Annales E.S.C.* 32 (1977): 1074-89. G. Duby, *Les trois ordres ou l'imaginaire de la féodalité du Moyen-âge,* (Paris 1979), pp. 163-68.

38. Text edited by R. M. Manselli, "Il monaco Enrico e la sua eresia," in *Bullettino dell'Instituto storico Italiano* 65 (1953): 36-62, who suggested the possibility of attributing it to William of Saint-Thierry — hypothesis considered "nonconclusive" by R. I. Moore, *The Birth of Popular Heresy* (New York 1975), p. 46. A specialist on William of Saint-Thierry, S. Ceglar, whom I consulted in a letter of May 27, 1977 suggested several observations in favor of Manselli's hypothesis which, it is to be hoped, will be published.

39. *Super Cantica,* 66, 3, *S. Bernardi opera,* II, (Rome 1958), p. 179. On the date and occasion of this sermon: *Recueil d'études sur S. Bernard,* I (Rome 1962), pp. 196-97 and 232.

40. *Super Cant.,* 66, 4-5, pp. 180-82.

41. *Super Cant.,* 66, 10, p. 185.

42. *Sermones contra Catharos,* 5, 2, *P.L.,* 197, 27 C-D.

43. Ibid., 28 A.

44. Ibid., 28 D.

45. Ibid., 29 B.

46. Ibid., 30 C.

47. Ibid., 30 B.

48. Ibid., 29 C.

49. Ibid., 30 A. On the sense of *venia,* see Chap. 2, n. 2.

50. Ibid., 30 C.

Chapter 2

1. *The Good of Marriage,* I, in *The Fathers of the Church,* (New York 1955), 27:9.

2. On the real meaning of *venia* in St. Augustine and tradition where the word means "indulgence" and not venial sin, see S. Princkaers, "Ce que le Moyen-âge pensait du mariage," in *La vie spirituelle* 82 (1967): 415-18. On the very complex doctrine of St. Augustine as a whole, excellent clarification by E. S. Ludovici, "Sessualità matrimonio e concupiscenza in Agustino," in *Etica sessuale e matrimonio nel cristianesimo delle origini,* ed., R. Cantelamessa (Milan 1976), pp. 212-72; this historian has the rare merit of taking into account both the chronology of Augustine's work and the evolution of his thought. On the dignity of the body and its activities according to St. Augustine, see H. I. Marrou, *Saint Augustine and the Augustinian Tradition* (Villanova, Penn. 1966). On *amor maritalis* in St. Augustine, see G. Armas, "Hacia una ética agostiniana del hogar," in *Augustinus* 3 (1958): 470-71.

3. On the way in which St. Jerome's personal difficulties and his refutation of Jovinian influenced his doctrine, there is a nuanced study by C. H. Nodet, "Position de S. Jérôme en face des problèmes sexuels," in *Mystique et continence, Etudes carmélitaines,* 1952, p. 308-56.

4. *De parentelae gradibus, P.L.,* 145, 193-94.

5. V. I. Flint, "The 'School of Laon': A Reconsideration," in *Recherches de Théologie Ancienne et Médiévale* 93 (1976): 107.

6. *De Sacramentis,* II, 99, 6, *P.L.,* 176, 688-94.

7. H. Weisweiler, "Maître Simon et son groupe. De Sacramentis" (Louvain 1937). Appendix: R. M. Martin, O.P., "Pierre le Mangeur. De Sacramentis," (Louvain 1937), pp. 47*, 51*, etc.; in O. Lottin, *Psychologie et morale aux XIIᵉ et XIIIᵉ siècles,* vol. 5, (Louvain 1959), pp. 105, 295, etc.; in H. Weisweiler, *Das Schrifttum der Schule Anselms von Laon und Wilhelms von Champeaux in Deutschen Bibliotheken. Ein Beitrag zur Geschichte der Verbreitung der ältesten scholastischen Schule in deutschen Landen* (Münster i.W. 1936), pp. 372, etc.; in the art. "Mariage," in *Dictionnaire de Théologie Catholique,* vol. 9, 2 (Paris 1927), col. 2147, (1154-56), and in other editions of Sentences.

8. Texts can be found in J. B. Molin and P. Mutembe, *Le rituel du mariage en France aux XIIᵉ-XIIIᵉ siècles* (Paris 1974), p. 291, etc.; in K. Ritzer, *Le mariage dans les Eglises chrétiennes du Iᵉʳ au XIᵉ siècle* (Paris 1970), p. 400, n. 644, and even before that in earlier rituals, ibid., pp. 447-50. The evolution of these rituals has been traced in a masterly way by M. Sheehan, "Choice of Marriage Partner in the Middle Ages: Development and Mode of Application of a Theory of Marriage," in *Studies in Medieval and Renaissance History,* vol. 1 (The University of British Columbia, 1978), pp. 27-32. Other appearances of *amor, dilectio, caritas* in the marriage rituals have been noted in medieval texts by P. Salmon, "Un témoin de la vie chrétienne dans l'Eglise de Rome au XIᵉ siècle: le 'Liber officialis' de la basilique des Saints Apôtres," in *Rivista di storia della Chiesa in Italia* 33 (1979): 67; E. Lodi, *Enchiridion euchologicum fontium liturgicarum* (Rome 1979), n. 1503, 2612, 2837-39, 3257. Recent bibliography on these texts and their sources in A. G. Martimort, *La documentation liturgique de D. Edmond Martene. Etude codicologique* (Vatican City, 1978) (*Studi e testi,* n. 279), n. 690-706, pp. 357-62. Certain

of these texts have been translated into French and presented by A. Gauvreau, *Rituels sacramentaires* (Montreal, 1966), pp. 114–20.

9. H. J. F. Reinhardt, *Die Ehelehre der Schule des Anselms von Laon. Eine theologie und kirchengeschichtliche Untersuchung zu den Ehetexten der frühen Pariser Schule des 12. Jahrhunderts.* Anhang: *Edition des Ehetraktates der Sententie Magistri A* (Münster 1974), p. 50.

10. Ibid., pp. 46, 130, etc.

11. On this treatise, entitled *De arbore parentele*, G. Miccoli, "Un nuovo manoscritto del Liber de vita christiana di Bonizone di Sutri," in *Studi Medievali* 3ᵃs., VII (1966): 390–98.

12. This fact had already been remarked upon by G. Le Bras, loc. cit., col. 2143.

13. Eligius Buytaert, ed., *Petri Abaelardi Opera*, 2 vols. (Turnhout 1969); *Sic et non*, c. 130, *P.L.* 178, 1560.

14. The formula is from G. Le Bras, *loc. cit.*, col. 2144.

15. Evidences have been given by P. Delhaye, "Le dossier antimatrimonial de l'Adversus Iovinianum et son influence sur quelques écrits latins du XIIᵉ siècle," in *Medieval Studies* 13 (1953): 74.

16. C. 31, *P.L.*, 178, 1745.

17. N. M. Häring, ed., *Sententiae Magistri Gisleberti Pictavicusis*, in *Archives d'histoire doctrinale et littéraire du Moyen-âge*, 53 e. année, 1978, (Paris 1979), pp. 152–62.

18. J. A. Brundage, "The Treatment of Marriage in the Quaestiones Londinenses (MS Royal 9. E. VII)," in *Manuscripta* 19 (1975): 86–97.

19. M. M. Sheehan, "The Formation and Stability of Marriage in Fourteenth Century England: Evidence of an Ely Register," in *Medieval Studies* 33 (1971): 228–63; "Choice of Marriage Partner", pp. 8–14. M. Sheehan has brought out the essential of all this evolution, due more to theologians than canonists: "There was a desire to internalize the marriage relationship. Theologians emphasized the bond of charity between the spouses and the possibility of its growth as a reason for their choice of each other . . . . The life of charity . . . was deeper and more permanent than sexual attraction . . . ."

20. C. N. L. Brooke, *Marriage in Christian History: An Inaugural Lecture* (Cambridge 1978), pp. 19–26.

21. *Monks and Love in Twelfth Century France*, pp. 8–26; "Il monachesimo femminile tra i secoli XII e XIII, in *Movimento religioso e Francescanesimo nel sec. XIII* (Assise 1980); and bibliography in P. Rousset, "La femme et la famille dans l' 'Histoire ecclésiastique' d'Orderic Vitalis," in *Zeitschrift für Schweizerische Kirchengeschichte* 63 (1969): 25.

22. Orderic Vitalis, *Historia ecclesiastica*, 1. V., ed. A. Le Prévost, (Paris 1840): 456–60.

23. Texts assembled under the title "La vêture ad succurrendum d'après le moine Raoul," in *Analecta monastica* 3 (*Studia Anselmiana* 37) (1955): 158–68.

24. On this sort of text, see P. Bec, *La lyrique française au Moyen-âge*, vol.

1 (Paris 1977), pp. 69–90; (Paris 1978), 2: 13–24. In the "Chansons de nonnes" said to be unhappy and quoted ibid., it is said that they are so because they had been "faites nonnes" in spite of themselves, when they were young; on this problem, which existed in the twelfth century and after in traditional monasticism, whereas the new orders endeavored to suppress it, cf. *II monachesimo femminile,* loc. cit.

25. Ch. V, par. 2.

26. The examples of Saint-Etienne of Troyes, Montier-la-Celle, Notre-Dame-aux-Nonnains are quoted by T. Evergates, *Feudal Society in the Baillage of Troyes under the Counts of Champagne 1152–1284* (Baltimore and London 1975), p. 23.

27. E. M. Makowski, "Marital Debt. The Development of a Canonistic History," in *Journal of Medieval History* 3 (1977): 99–114.

28. S. Augustin, *De civ. Dei,* 15, 16, CC 48, p. 478, 85; Gratien, *Decretum,* 1, C. 35, q. I. Cf. J. T. Noonan, Jr., "Power to Choose," in *Viator* 4 (1973): 429.

29. "Sciendum est duo genera esse coniugii, unum inculpabile, aliud cum culpa veniali" (Praeloquia, 2, 5, *P.L.,* 136, 191 C).

30. "Vos quoque laici . . . liceat Christo coniugati innocenter vivere . . ." (*Chronicon,* 8, 34, *M.G., Script. rer. Germ.,* N.S., IX, 1935, pp. 495–96.

31. "Commixtio enim carnalis viri et femine peccatum esset, nisi statum coniugatorum suscepissent" (*Quaestiones de Epistolis Pauli,* ed. R. M. Martin, *Oeuvres de Robert de Melun,* 2 (Louvain 1938), 2: 196, 19.

32. "Constat nonnulla nec fieri sine gloria et posse fieri sine culpa, ideoque, si fiant, digna esse paemiis, non tamen suppliciis si non fiant. Nam et non tangere mulierens (1 Cor. 7: 1), meriti est non mediocris, et nullius tamen delicti propriam amplecti conjugem" (*De praecepto et dispensatione,* 42, *S. Bernardi opera,* III, p. 282). We may also quote this text of Alan of Lille (d. 1203 at Cîteaux), *De fide contra haereticos,* I. 64: "Concedimus etiam conjugium non posse consummari sine carnali coitu, verum carnalis coitus non semper peccatum est; nam per conjugii sacramentum fit, ut carnale commercium aut grave non sit peccatum, aut omnino peccatum non sit", *P.L.,* 210, 366.

33. On this subject, texts are compared in *Monks and Love,* p. 120.

34. C. Violante, "Discorso conclusivo," in *Il matrimonio nella società altomedievale* (Spoleto 1977), p. 992.

35. Texts are quoted by R. Javelet, *Image et ressemblance au XIIᵉ siècle. De S. Anselme à Alain de Lille* (Paris 1967), 1: 239; 2: 208–11.

36. R. Javelet, ibid., p. 241. The author remarks elsewhere, p. 242, that the teaching of Abelard on this point had little influence.

37. *Epist.,* VIII, T. P. McLaughlin, ed., "Abelard's Rule for Religious Women," in *Medieval Studies* 18 (1956): 241–92. On this Rule written by Abelard for the Paraclete: " 'Ad ipsam sophiam Christum' Le témoignage monastique d'Abélard," in *Revue d'ascétique et de mystique* 46 (1970): 172–76.

38. "Peter Abelard: Planctus and Satire." in *Poetic Individuality in the*

Middle Ages. New Departures in Poetry. 1000–1150 (Oxford 1970), pp. 114–49. The antifeminist passage of the *planctus* is reproduced p. 122.

39. Numerous witnesses of this secular antifeminist poetry in A. Wulff, *Die frauenfeindlichen Dichtungen in den romanischen Literaturen des Mittelalters* (Halle 1914).

40. Sheehan, "Choice of Marriage Partner", pp. 24–25.

41. Ibid., pp. 32–33; p. 25: "It is clear that thinking on marriage was diffused to the level of personal instruction by the early years of the thirteenth century."

Chapter 3

1. On the date of this work, see R. Baron, "Hugues de Saint-Victor," in *Dictionnaire de spiritualité*, vol. 7, part 1 (1969), col. 912. On the importance of the doctrinal contribution of Hugh, see G. Fransen, in *Le lien matrimonial.* Colloque du Cerdic. Strasbourg, 21–23 Mai 1970, published by R. Metz-J. Schlick, (Strasbourg 1970), p. 114–15.

2. *De virginitate Beatae Mariae, P.L.,* 176, 866.

3. Ibid., 859.

4. Ibid., 860.

5. Gen. 2: 24; Mt. 19: 5.

6. *P.L.,* 176, 864.

7. Ibid., 874–75.

8. Ibid., 876.

9. *Cant., 4,* 9.

10. *Cant., 8,* 7.

11. G. Dumeige, ed., *De IV gradibus violentae caritatis, Yves. Epître à Séverin sur la charité. Richard de Saint-Victor. Les quatre degrés de la violente charité* (Paris 1955), pp. 127–77. According to G. Dumeige, *Richard de Saint-Victor et l'idée chrétienne de l'amour* (Paris 1952), p. 170, the date is uncertain. The texts are quoted here from Clare Kirchbergen, ed. and trans., *Richard of Saint Victor. Selected Writings on Contemplation.* (New York: Harper and Brothers, n. d.), p. 213.

12. Ibid., p. 220.

13. Ibid., p. 215.

14. Ibid.

15. Ibid., p. 220.

16. R. J. Cormier, *One Heart and One Mind. The Rebirth of Virgil's Hero in Medieval French Romance* (University of Mississippi, 1973), p. 255.

17. *Scivias,* 1, 2, 10–12, CC, 43, pp. 18–21 and passim.

18. *Epist.,* I, 21, *Ad abbatissam reclusam, P.L.,* 171, 195 D.

19. *De arte praedicandi,* c. 45, *P.L.,* 210, 193.

20. *Epist.,* 9, *P.L.,* 211, 610; on measure, col. 611. In these texts, as other authors do elsewhere, Adam of Perseigne uses the expression *torus immaculatus* with the meaning of faithful marriage, as in the Letter to the Hebrews (13: 4).

21. Alan of Lille, *De arte praedicandi*, 45, *P.L.*, 210, 193.
22. D. L. Dorrie and H. Farmen, eds., *The Life of St. Hugh of Lincoln* (London 1961), pp. 46–48.
23. Pseudo-Anselm, *Carmen de contemptu mundi*, *P.L.*, 158, 697.
24. *De nuptiis*, *P.L.*, 176, 1201–18.
25. J. Leclercq, ed., *Hélinand de Froidmont ou Odon de Chériton?* in *Archives d'histoire doctrinale et littéraire du Moyen-Âge*, 40 (Paris 1966): 67.
26. The question has been asked by J. Van Engen in *Speculum* 53 (1978): 574–75, in a review of the work by R. Goy, *Die Überlieferung der Werke Hugos von St. Viktor: Ein Betrag zur Kommunikationsgeschichte im Mittelalter* (Stuttgart 1976). On the compared traditions of St. Bernard and of Hugh of Saint-Victor: F. Masai, "Sur la tradition manuscrite de deux lettres-traités de S. Bernard," forthcoming in *Mélanges*.
27. Cf. M. Maccarone, art. "Innocent III," in *Dictionnaire de spiritualité*, VII, 2 (1971), col. 1768.
28. *De quadripartita specie nuptiarum. Epithalamium in laudem sponsi et sponsae*, *P.L.*, 217, 921–68.
29. The elements of the ritual are indicated in J. Gaudemet, "Le lien matrimonial. Les incertitudes du Moyen-Âge," in *Revue de droit canonique* 21 (1971): 90–91.
30. *P.L.*, 217, 930 D.
31. E. Makowski "Marital Debt," art. cit. Even before he was pope, in his treatise *De miseria humanae conditionis*, Innocent III had given a somber picture of everything, including marital union, without, however, seeing it as sinful: ed. M. Maccarone, (Lugano 1955), p. 10 (l.III,1).

Chapter 4

1. Philip of Harvengt, *Vita B. Odae Virginis*, *P.L.* 203, 1359–74.
2. C. H. Talbot, ed. and trans., *The Life of Christina of Markyate. A Twelfth Century Recluse* (Oxford 1959).
3. B. de Gaiffier, "Intactam sponsam relinquens. A propos de la Vie de S. Alexis," in *Analecta Bollandiana* 65 (1947): 157, 195; R. Gregoire, "Il matrimonio mistico," in *Il matrimonio nella società altomedievale* (Spoleto 1977), pp. 758–78.
4. Radbord of Utrecht, *Tomellus de S. Amalberga* in *Acta SS. Bolland.*, Iul. III, (1723), p. 89, n. 4.
5. A. Beer, *Heinrich Herrscher und Heiliger* (Freiburg im Breisgau 1939); A. Albrecht, *Heinrich und Kunigunde. Deutungsversuche für unsere Zeit* (Bamberg 1978), with reproductions of sculptures in the cathedral of Bamberg representing the life of Henry and Cunegund.
6. H. Günter, *Kaiser Heinrich II, der Heilige* (Kempis and Munich 1904), p. 11; a sculpture of the tomb of Henry at Bamberg is also reproduced ibid., p. 44.
7. J. B. Sägemuller, "Die Ehe Heinrich des II., des Heiligen mit

Kunigunde," in *Theologische Quartalschrift* 87 (1905): 75–95; ibid., 89 (1907): 564–77; idem, "Das 'impedimentum impotentiae' bei der Frau von Alexander III," ibid. 93 (1911): 90–126; idem, "Nochmals das 'impedimentum impotentiae' bei der Frau von Alexander III," ibid. 95 (1913): 565–611. Whether there was impotence, the literary tradition created by the *Additamentum* which will be dealt with shortly, existed and was used, for example by Joachim of Fiore: cf. F. Pelster, S. J., "Ein Elogium Joachim von Fiore auf Kaiser Heinrich II und seine Gemahlin die Heilige Kunigunde," in *Liber Floridus. Mittellateinische Studien Paul Lehman. gewidmet,* hrsgb. v. B. Bischoff-S. Brechter, (Sankt Ottilien 1950), 6: 340–41; the use which is made by R. Glaber is quoted by B. de Gaiffier, "Intactam sponsam relinquens," p. 178, n. 6.

8. Ed. *M. G. H., SS,* IV, p. 821–28, reproduced in *P.L.* 140, 187–98; the text will be quoted here after this edition; it is given as being of the beginning of the thirteenth century in BHL 3814. The words *amor* and *amare* recur seven times in the passage found in *P.L.,* 140, 190 C–191 A.

9. Ibid., 194 C.

10. Ibid., 194 C–D.

11. Ibid., 187.

12. A. Riese, ed., *Historia Apollonii Regis Tyri* (Leipzig 1893), col. 23, p. 42. On this text and its posterity, see M. Manitius, *Geschichte der lateinischen Literatur des Mittelalters* (Munich 1959), 1: 614–16; bibliography in F. Brunholz, art. "Apollonius von Tyros," in *Lexikon für Theologie und Kirche,* I, (Fribourg 1957), col. 720.

13. C. Gnädinger, *Eremitica. Studien zur altfranzösischen Heiligenvitae des 12. und 13. Jahrhunderts* (Tübingen 1972), pp. 45–50.

14. U. Mölk, ed., "Die älteste lateinische Alexiusvita (9./10. Jarhhundert)," in *Romanisches Jahrbuch* 17 (1976): 305.

15. R. Robertson, *Poem and Spirit: the Twelfth-Century French Life of Mary the Egyptian,* forthcoming. I thank the author for having communicated the text.

16. Ed. *Acta SS. Boll.,* Iul. V, (1727), p. 667–727; cf. M. Coens, in *Analecta Bollandiana,* 76 (1958), p. 262–64.

17. *Ed. cited* n. 141, p. 700.

18. Ibid., n. 113–114, p. 693–94.

19. *Acta SS. Boll.,* Iun. IV (1707), n. 12, pp. 639–40.

20. Ibid., n. 14, p. 640.

21. J. C. Poulin, *L'idéal de la sainteté dans l'Aquitaine carolingienne d'après les sources hagiographiques (750–950)* (Université Laval, Quebec 1975), pp. 138–39.

22. Ed. *Acta. SS. Boll.,* Sept. II (1748), 260–69.

23. Ed. *M.G. SS,* 30, 2, pp. 912–17.

24. "Concessa quae pro utensium modo vel bona esse possunt vel mala, in quibus est saeculi usus, coniugii voluptas, carnium esus, molliorum et cultiorum indumentorum apparatus". Agius, *Vita Haithumodae* (written circa 874), ed. *MG, SS,* IV, pp. 166–75, n. 7.

25. *Acta SS. Boll.*, Mart. II (1618), p. 358–70. In the *Life* of Count Gerald of Aurillac, written by St. Odo of Cluny (c. 920) and which is considered a "monastic model," we see that it is during nocturnal prayer that he was asked to approach his wife in order to have a son: "In ipso coniugio sese castificari tantoper studebat, ut semoto frequenter a coniuge toro, solus accubitaret, velut ad tempus, iuxta Apostolum, orationi vacans. Quadam vero nocte, monitus in somnis perhibetur, quatenus uxorem cognosceret, quia filius generaturus esset. . . Cognovit itaque uxorem. . ." (*Vita Geraldi*, 2, *P.L.*, 133, 643). Later, St. Louis IX of France, in the course of the nights of voluntary continence which he spent with his wife, contented himself with walking up and down in their room, according to E. R. Labande, "Quelques traits du caractère du roi S. Louis," in *Revue d'histoire de la spiritualité* 50 (1974): 143.

26. *Acta SS. Boll.*, Jan. II (1698), pp. 328–35.

27. *Acta SS. Boll.*, April I (1675), pp. 670–71.

28. "Ambo pariter in religione coniugali honeste conversantes, ad Domini servitium et eorum solatium quinque filios divini muneris largitate genuerunt" (*Vita S. Gaufridi*, ed. *Anal. Bolland.*, I [1882], col. 1, p. 392).

29. After *Ide de Lorraine, comtesse de Boulogne, Une vie sainte en des temps difficiles. 1043–1113*. Preface by Dom P. Grammont, Bénédictines, Bayeux, s.d. (1979), pp. 20–22.

30. In his *Epist.* 53 (G. Constable, ed., *The Letters of Peter the Venerable* [Cambridge, Mass. 1967], p. 159), Peter the Venerable describes the sadness of his mother, Raingarde, when her husband died; she thus continued to show that she was "a faithful spouse." William of Saint-Thierry explains too how Aleth, the mother of St. Bernard, reconciled herself as much as she could (*in quantum poterat*) to the state she had assumed (*assumptae professionis*) with a life of prayer and good works: *Vita prima S. Bernardi*, I, 5, *P.L.*, 185, 229–30. In such texts, the expression *thorus immaculatus* retains the meaning it had been given in the Bible and tradition: a marriage free from adultery.

Chapter 5

1. F. C. Tubach, *Index exemplorum. A Handbook of Medieval Religious Tales* (Helsinki 1969).

2. The affinities existing between exempla and fabliaux have been pointed out by G. F. Lacy, "Augustinian Imagery and Fabliau 'Obscenity' " in *Studies on the Seven Sages of Rome and Other Essays in Medieval Literature dedicated to the Memory of Jean Misrahi*, ed. H. Niedzielski, Education Research Association, (Honolulu 1978), pp. 219–30, and G. R. Mermier, *D'un chapitre du "De Miseria Humanae Conditionis" du Pape Innocent III aux "Quinze joies du Mariage"*, ibid., p. 234.

3. P. N. Carter, ed., "An Edition of William of Malmesbury's Treatise on the Miracles of the Virgin Mary" (Ph.D. thesis, Oxford University 1959), pp. 194–98, 418–81.

4. Ibid., pp. 197–204, 488–92.
5. Ibid., pp. 258, 580–82.
6. *De miraculis B. Mariae Virginis*, C. 2, *P.L.*, 173, 1382–83.
7. *De laude S. Mariae*, C. 13, *P.L.*, 156, 573–74.
8. Under the title "Pétulance et spiritualité dans le Commentaire d'Hélinand sur le Cantique des cantiques," in *Archives d'histoire doctrinale et littéraire du Moyen-Âge* 31 (1964): 55, I have edited this text. On the author: "Hélinand de Froidmont ou Odon de Chériton?" ibid. 32 (1965): 61–69.
9. Leclercq, "Pétulance" p. 55.
10. Ibid., p. 53.
11. *Equity and Compassion in Papal Marriage Decretals to England*, forthcoming in *Proceedings* of the Colloque held at Louvain in 1978 on *Love and Marriage in the Twelfth Century*.
12. M. M. Sheehan, review of the work mentioned in the following note, in *Speculum* 52 (1977): 983–87.
13. R. H. Helmholz, *Marriage Litigation in Medieval England* (Cambridge and New York 1974).
14. Sheehan, loc. cit., p. 985.
15. Ibid., p. 986.
16. Ibid., p. 987.
17. Helmholz, *Marriage*, p. 7.
18. Ibid., p. 32.
19. Ibid., p. 72.
20. Ibid., p. 91.
21. Ibid., p. 131.
22. Ibid., p. 205.
23. Ibid., p. 102.
24. Cited ibid., p. 13, n. 20.

Chapter 6

1. A survey of the problems concerning courtly love is to be found in R. Boase, *The Origin and Meaning of Courtly Love. A Critical Study of European Scholarship* (Manchester 1977). In the following pages, there will be no attempt to study a field which competent specialists are already examining, but simply, with a few examples, to try to situate it with regard to another set of facts in literary productions which are equally vast.
2. *Marriage in Christian History. An Inaugural Lecture* (Cambridge 1978), p. 21.
3. Rightly, P. Bec, *La lyrique française au Moyen-âge*, vol. 1 (Paris 1977), pp. 30–34, distinguishes two registers, one "popularizing" and the other "aristocratizing". In both instances, the manuscript tradition does not seem to indicate that secular writings on love were widely diffused in the twelfth century. Likewise, there are but few manuscripts for the fabliaux, as is evident from the facts given by P. Menard, *Fabliaux français du Moyen-âge*, vol. 1

(Paris 1979). Moreover, in the fabliaux, the adulterer is generally ridiculed, whereas the faithful partner is avenged. On the question of the reciprocal influence of romances on their readers and of society on authors, see J. C. Payen, F. N. M. Diekstro, et. al., *Le roman (Typologie des sources du Moyen-âge occidental* 12), (Turnhout 1979), pp. 24–29, 122–23 and passim. According to J. C. Rivière, *Pastourelles,* vol. 1 (Geneva 1974), p. 15, "on 120 documents finally found, 85 are *ùnica,*" and even for the others, the manuscripts are of the restricted number of eighteen, according to the list given on pp. 178–79; these love poems were only preserved then in a few collections and these were not widely diffused.

4. J. Deroy, "Thèmes et termes de la fin' amor dans les *Sermones super Cantica canticorum* de Saint Bernard de Clairvaux," in *Actes du XIIe Congrès International de Linguistique et Philologie romanes* (Quebec: University of Laval, 1976), p. 855.

5. At least the summary distributed under the title "Amour et mariage, amour hors mariage: tensions et problèmes dans la littérature française du XIIe siècle" contains these sentences: "It would be wrong to believe that marriage is a contested institution, that unbridled and lawless love is universally glorified and naively solemnized. In the same texts, marriage seems to be a sure value, a refuge value . . . . If love outside marriage prevails over loveless marriage, it appears that marriage for reasons of love is for our authors a constant ideal."

6. P. Ménard, *Les lais de Marie de France* (Paris 1979), p. 134.

7. Ibid., p. 141.

8. In *Monks and Love,* I had already devoted a few pages (115–18) to Andrew the Chaplain, before being able to consult the works the results of which will be summarized here and which, in fact, confirm the indications I gave, at the same time as they considerably explicate and complete them.

9. A. Karnein, 'Auf der Suche nach einem Autor: Andreas, Verfasser von "De Amore" ', *Germanische-Romanische Monatsschrift,* N.F., Bd. 28, 1978, p. 2.

10. Ibid., pp. 4–6.

11. P. Dronke, review of *André le Chapelain: Traité de l'amour courtois,* trans. Claude Buridant, (Paris 1974), in *Medium Aevum* 45 (1975): 320.

12. Ibid., p. 318.

13. A. Karnein, *De Amore Deutsch, Der Tractatus des Andreas Capellanus in der Übersetzung Johann Hartliebs* (Munich 1970), pp. 22–23.

14. A. Karnein, *Auf der Suche,* p. 15.

15. Ibid., p. 1.

16. "Die falsche Liebe" (Karnein, *Auf der Suche,* p. 15).

17. P. Lehmann, *Die Parodie im Mittelalter* (Munich 1922), pp. 154–71.

18. R. J. Schoek, "Andreas Capellanus and St. Bernard of Clairvaux: The Twelve Rules of Love and the Twelve Steps of Humility," in *Modern Language Notes* 66 (1951): 295–300.

19. It will do to give a few examples: "Est igitur primo videre quid sit amor,

et unde . . . et quis sit affectus . . ." (E. Trojel, ed., *Andreae Capellani Regis Francorum De amore libri tres* [Copenhagen 1892], p. 2). "Hoc autem est praecipue notandum, quod . . ." (ibid., p. 6). "Est nunc videre quae sint . . ." (ibid., p. 11, etc.) In fact, according to Drouart de la Vache, cited *ibid.*, p. XVI, the text contains the objections of the disciple and the answers of the master, as in a *disputatio* in due form.

20. Ibid., p. 359.

21. Ibid., pp. 150–55; Betsy Bowden, "The Art of Courtly Copulation," in *Medievalia et Humanistica: Studies in Medieval and Renaissance Culture,* n.s. 9 (1979): 67–85, has given a recent bibliography on Andrew the Chaplain. Insistence has been laid on the erotic nature of his vocabulary and his play on words, yet leaving open certain questions about the author. But the scarcity of popular tradition seems to suggest an answer in the negative to the question about the *De amore* being popular.

22. *Il monachesimo femminile fra i secoli XII e XIII,* forthcoming; article *Nobiltà,* in *Dizionario degli Istituti di Perfezione,* V, Rome 1979.

23. This insistence of the *De amore* on the social categories has been stressed by G. Duby, *Les trois ordres ou l'imaginaire de la féodalité* (Paris 1979), pp. 404–13; cf. also *Monks and Love,* pp. 116–18.

24. All these facts have been admirably clarified by P. Toubert, "La théorie du mariage chez les moralistes carolingiens," in *Il matrimonio nella società altomedievale* (Spoleto 1977), pp. 233–85.

25. Ed. in "Les Munimenta fidei de S. Benoît d'Aniane," in *Analecta monastica,* I (*Studia Anselmiana* 20), (Rome 1946), p. 56.

26. "Ecrits spirituels de l'école de Jean de Fécamp," in *Analecta monastica,* ibid., pp. 91–114; *Un maître de la vie spirituelle au XIe. siècle,* (Paris 1946).

27. The influence of Benedict of Aniane and especially Jean of Fécamp in these two domains has been stressed by L. Pollmann, *Die Liebe in der hochmittelalterliche Literatur Frankreichs* (Frankfurt 1966), pp. 220–21.

28. "Nam et qui, verbi gratia, uxorem habet speciosam, petulanti oculo vel animo respicit pulchriorem" (*De diligendo Deo,* 18, *S. Bernardi opera,* III, p. 134, 18–19.

29. Ibid., 19, p. 135, 24; 20, p. 136.

30. *S. Bernard et l'antiféminisme du XIIe. siècle,* forthcoming.

31. R. Arnaldez, "Statut juridique et social de la femme en Islam," in *Cahiers de civilisation médiévale* 20 (1977): 143.

Chapter 7

1. *Super Cantica,* 1, 8–12. The *Sermones super Cantica* are in vols. 1 and 2 of the *S. Bernardi opera* (Rome 1957–58). In the following notes, the references which are not preceded by an abbreviation refer to this work: the first figure indicates the sermon, the following figures indicate the numbers of the paragraph within the sermon.

2. *Monks and Love,* pp. 9–16.
3. 16, 9.
4. *Monks and Love,* pp. 17–18.
5. 2, 3.
6. 9, 4.
7. 9, 7–8.
8. 9, 9.
9. 10, 3.
10. 10, 1.
11. 4, 1.
12. 8, 7–8.
13. *De diversis,* 89, 2, *S. Bernardi opera,* VI, 1, p. 336.
14. 14, 4. The expression *praerepta oscula* which Bernard uses here was in Lucretius, *De nat. rer.,* 3, 896.
15. 14, 5.
16. An example of the texts evoked here is the poem "Pauca loquar . . .," in Bruce Harbert, ed., *A Thirteenth Century Anthology of Rhetorical Poems* (Toronto 1975), pp. 11–12.
17. 2, 2.
18. 45, 1.
19. 61, 2.
20. 14, 5.
21. 7, 2.
22. 22, 3.
23. 7, 4.
24. 8, 9.
25. 9, 1.
26. 23, 1–2.
27. 23, 9.
28. 23, 10.
29. 81, 1.
30. 83, 1.
31. 83, 3.
32. Mt. 19: 5.
33. 83, 5.
34. 83, 6.
35. 85, 12.
36. *Brevis commentatio super Cantica canticorum,* 4, *P.L.* 184, 411.
37. 84, 6.
38. 84, 7.
39. 65, 5.
40. 65, 6.
41. 66, 1.
42. 66, 3.
43. 66, 4.
44. 85, 12–13.

45. On the Trinitarian metaphor of the kiss in St. Augustine, see N. I. Perella, *An Interpretative History of Kiss Symbolism and Related Religio-Erotic Themes* (Berkeley and Los Angeles 1969), pp. 46–50, and with more details, especially in connection with St. Fulgentius, B. de Margerie, *La Trinité chrétienne dans l'histoire* (Paris 1975), pp. 48–53.

46. De Margerie, *La Trinité*, pp. 54–55.
47. Ibid., p. 383.
48. Ibid., p. 380.
49. Ibid., pp. 375–86.
50. L. H. Parias, *Trois entretiens avec Pierre Bellego* (Paris 1978), p. 65.
51. H. U. von Balthasar, *Adrienne von Speyer et sa mission théologique* (Paris 1978), p. 107.
52. De Margerie, *La Trinité*, pp. 412–15.
53. Ibid., p. 56.
54. 8, 1.
55. 8, 2.
56. 8, 5.
57. 8, 6.
58. 8, 7.
59. 8, 8.
60. *De diversis*, 89, 1, *S. Bernardi opera*, VI, 1.
61. De Margerie, *La Trinité*, p. 57.
62. This is the case in *Les stances de Bhaztrihari*, trans. M. Lalore, s.l. n.d., p. 15.
63. 80, 8.
64. *De consideratione*, 5, 22, *S. Bernardi opera*, III, pp. 484–85. All that has just been said about the Fathers and St. Bernard does not imply that they were the last word about speculative theology on the Trinity such as it was elaborated by St. Thomas, as H. Dondaine, O.P., has remarked, quoted by Y. Congar, *Je crois en l'Esprit Saint, I. L'expérience de l'Esprit* (Paris 1979), I, p. 129. Dondaine adds elsewhere (p. 130): "Thus it is enlightening—and very interesting—to present the Holy Spirit as the Friendship of the Father and the Son, the mutual Love of Father and Son."
65. 2, 2.
66. 2, 3.
67. 2, 3.
68. 2, 9.
69. 12, 11.
70. 45, 1.
71. 45, 7.
72. 45, 8.
73. 68, 4.
74. 82, 8.
75. 85, 13.
76. 64, 3–4.

77. 61, 7.
78. 61, 8.
79. *Epist.*, 126, 6, *S. Bernardi opera*, VII, pp. 313–14.
80. *S. Bernardi opera*, I, p. 46, 26–27; II, p. 302, 20; VII, p. 314, 4. On the original meaning of the verse of Genesis which is quoted in all these cases, see M. Gilbert, "Une seule chair," (Gen. 2: 24), in *Nouvelle revue théologique* 110 (1978): 66–89.
81. *De consideratione*, 5, 18, *S. Bernardi opera*, III, p. 489, 21.
82. *De diversis* 70, *S. Bernardi opera*, VI, 1, p. 320, 11.
83. 59, 2.
84. 83, 6.
85. G. R. Evans, "St. Anselm's images of Trinity," in *Journal of Theological Studies* 27 (1976): 46–57.
86. T. Moritz, "The Metaphor of Marriage in the Spiritual Writings of William of Saint-Thierry," in *Cistercian Studies* 11 (1976): 303.
87. De Margerie, *La Trinité*, pp. 50–52.
88. Gilbert De Hoyland, *In Cantica*, Serm. 2, 1, *P.L.*, 184, 17–18.
89. Under the title "Sommeil vigilant," in *Chances de la spiritualité occidentale* (Paris 1966), pp. 308–9, I have quoted texts.
90. *Serm.* 18, 2.
91. *Serm.* 21, 6.
92. *Serm.* 30, 1.
93. *Serm.* 31, 1; 32, 3; 37, 3; 40, 6.
94. *Monks and Love in Twelfth Century France*, pp. 33–37.

Chapter 8

1. On prostitution in the Old Testament and in the times of Jesus, see S. Legasse, "Jésus et les prostituées," in *Revue théologique de Louvain* 7 (1976): 137–42 (in particular, on conversion of the sinner in Lk. 7: 36–50, ibid., pp. 142–54). Art. πόρνη in *Theological Dictionary of the New Testament*, ed. by G. Friedrich, (Grand Rapids 1969), 6: 579–95. The signification of Hosea and Gomer is particularly important in the Old Testament (cf. J. L. Mays, *Hosea: A Commentary*, [Philadelphia 1969] and in St. Matthew, D. Hill, "On the Use and Meaning of Hosea VI, 6, in Matthew's Gospel," in *New Testament Studies* 24 [1977]: 107–19).
2. Heb. 11: 31.
3. Jos., 2: 11 and 6: 17.
4. C. Spicq, *Épître aux Hébreux* (Paris 1953), 2: 361–62.
5. Pr. 7: 7–9.
6. Texts are assembled and commented by H. U. von Balthasar, "Casta meretrix," in *Sponsa Verbi, Skizzen zur Theologie*, (Einsiedeln 1961) 2: 203–305. What was first a theological theme became from Salvian onward, in the fifth century, a historical observation according to C. Leonardi, "Alle

origini della cristianità medievale: Giovanni Cassiano e Slaviano di Marsiglia," in *Studi medievali* 18 (1977): 1149–1551: *La Chiesa meretrice*.

7. Cf. *Vie des Saints et des Bienheureux*, by the *RR. PP. Bénédictins de Paris*, 12 (Paris 1956): 201, and bibliography pp. 211–13.

8. "Meretrices autem dicuntur a merendo, i.c. promerendo stipendia libidinis" (Isidore de Seville, *Differentiae*, I, 263, *P.L.*, 83, 37).

9. C. Scaglioni, "Ideale coniugale e familiare in San Giovanni Crisostomo," in *Etica sessuale e matrimonio nel cristianesimo delle origini*, ed. R. Cantalamessa (Milan 1976), p. 370, pp. 368–78.

10. *"Joculator et saltator"*. *S. Bernard et l'image du jongleur dans les manuscrits*, in *Translatio studii. Manuscript and Library Studies honoring Oliver L. Kapsner*, O.S.B., (Collegeville, Minn. 1973), pp. 124–48, texts, iconography and bibliography on this immense category of medieval amusers. In a study in preparation, I shall give further information concerning converted harlots.

11. Cited by J. W. Baldwin, *Masters, Princes and Merchants: The Social Views of Peter the Chanter and his Circle* (Princeton 1970), 2: 140, n. 200.

12. In a forthcoming study, I shall return to these facts and texts.

13. M. Mollat, *Les pauvres au Moyen-âge. Etude sociale* (Paris 1978), pp. 98–105.

14. J. Daoust, art. "Fontevrault," in *Dictionnaire d'histoire et de géographie ecclésiastique*, 17 (1971), col. 961, with bibliography.

15. J. von Walther, *Vital de Savigny*, trans. J. Cahoud (n. p., n. d.), p. 19. M. D. Lenglet, "Biographie du Bˣ· Giraud de Sales," in *Cîteaux. Commentarii Cistercienses* 29 (1978): 27.

16. Texts and facts in Baldwin, *Masters*, vol. 1, pp. 133–37; ibid., vol. 2, pp. 91–95.

17. J. A. Brundage, "Prostitution in the Medieval Canon Law," in *Signs. Journal of Women in Culture and Society* I (1976): 827.

18. Ibid., pp. 842–43. Conversion is always hoped to be possible and could lead harlots to lawful marriage: J. A. Brundage, "Rape and Marriage in the Medieval Canon Law," in *Revue de droit canonique* 28 (1978): 71–72.

19. All these examples are cited in F. C. Tubach, *Index exemplorum: A Handbook of Medieval Religious Tales* (Helsinki 1969), pp. 454–55.

20. See above.

21. Cesarius of Heisterbach, *Dialogus miraculorum*, ed. J. Strange (Cologne, Bonn and Brussels 1851), dist. 8, chap. 53, pp. 125–26.

22. Ibid., dist. 12, chap. 20, p. 330.

23. Lk. 7: 36–50. On this text, see J. Delobel, "L'onction par la pécheresse. La composition littéraire de Lc 7, 36–50," in *Ephemerides theologicae Lovamienses* 42 (1966): 415–75; G. Bouwman, "La pécheresse hospitaliére" (Lk. 7: 36–50), ibid. 45 (1969): 172–79; J. Delobel, "Encore la pécheresse: Quelques réflexions critiques," ibid.: 180–83; E. Charpentier, *Le prophète ami des pécheurs (Lc. 7: 36–8, 3*, in *Assemblées du Seigneur*, 42 (11e. dimanche ordinaire), (Paris 1970), pp. 80–94.

24. On the identification of the three Marys, on the origin and the

development of devotion to Magdalen, recent synthesis, with bibliography, in P. M. Guillaume, art. "Marie-Madeleine (Sainte)" in *Dictionnaire de spiritualité*, fasc. 66–67, (Paris 1978), col. 559–75. The three Marys had already been identified by the Gnostics as is witnessed to by certain Apocrypha: J. Dart, *The Laughing Savior: The Discovery and Significance of the Nag Hammadi Gnostic Library* (New York 1976), pp. 127–78. On Magdalen in premedieval and postmedieval history: M. M. Malven, *Venus in Sackloth. The Magdalen's Origins and Metamorphoses* (Carbondale and Edwardsville 1975).

25. *Hom. in Evang.*, 25, *P.L.*, 76, 1188–91. St. Gregory applied to St. Scholastica a reminiscence of the sinner in Luke, in his *Dialogues*, II, 33, as has been shown by A. de Vogüe, "La rencontre Benoît-Scholastique," in *Revue d'histoire de la spiritualité* 48 (1972): 265–67.

26. For example, Smaragdus, *Collectiones in Epistolas et Evangelia, P.L.*, 102, 276; Haymon, *Homiliae de tempore*, 79, *P.L.*, 118, 484–87; Rabanus Maurus, *Homiliae in Evangelia et epistolas*, IV, *P.L.*, 110, 141. From the study of H. Barré, *Les homéliaires carolingiens de l'Ecole d'Auxerre* (Vatican City 1962), it is evident that the texts on Mary Magdalen are not numerous: they concern Easter and not the feast of Mary Magdalen, and St. Gregory is cut down: see, for example, p. 121. Inventory of the sermons on Mary Magdalen at Easter on pp. 337–38.

27. *Sermo II, In veneratione S. Mariae Magdalenae, P.L.*, 133, 714–21.

28. The expression is by V. Saxer, art. "Maria Magdalena, santa," in *Bibliotheca sanctorum*, 8 (Rome 1967), col. 1089.

29. The history of the cult of St. Mary Magdalen is known principally through the works of V. Saxer, the last one of which offers a synthesis: "Les ossements dits de Ste. Marie-Madeleine conservés à Saint-Maximin-la-Sainte-Baume," in *La Provence historique* 27 (1977): 257–302. Good summary of the history of the translation of the relics to Vézelay in P. J. Geary, *Furta Sacra: Thefts of Relics in the Central Middle Ages* (Princeton 1978), pp. 90–95.

30. This has been illustrated by P. Salmon, "La composition d'un Libellus precum à l'époque de la Réforme grégorienne," in *Benedictina* 26 (1979): 291–96.

31. *Oratio 16*, ed. F. S. Schmitt, *S. Anselmi Cantuariensis archiepiscopi opera omnia*, (Edinburgh 1946), 3: 65.

32. *Homiliae*, I, 25, *In festo B. Mariae Magdalenae, P.L.*, 155, 1398–1400.

33. *Allegoriae in Novum Testamentum*, 4, *P.L.*, 175, 816.

34. Pseudo-Hildebert, *Sermones de sanctis*, 69, *P.L.* 171, 675–78. The idea that the name Mary, which, according to its traditional etymology means "star of the sea," is applicable to Magdalen was developed by St. Odo, loc. cit., *P.L.*, 135, 721; it was taken up again in a twelfth-century English sermon, edited by R. Morris, *English Homilies of the Twelfth Century* (London 1973), pp. 140–42.

35. *Speculum Ecclesiae, De s. Maria Magdalena, P.L.*, 172, 979–82. The

expression of "worldly life" has also been given as the title of one of the ancient biographies of Mary Magdalen: V. Saxer, *Le dossier Vézelien de Marie Madeleine. Invention et translation des reliques en 1265-1267* (Brussels 1975), p. 16.

36. Saxer, *Le dossier Vézelien*, pp. 43, 47, 184 (n. 3), 203-4.

37. J. Szöverffy, ed., *Peter Abelard's "Hymnarius Paraclitensis"* (Albany 1975), p. 11.

38. Pierre de Blois, *Sermo 30, P.L.,* 207, 650.

39. *Super Cantica,* 14, 5.

40. 10, 6.

41. 10, 9.

42. 12, 7.

43. 12, 8.

44. 22, 9.

45. 25, 3-5; 26, 2.

46. *In Assumptione,* 3, 2, *S. Bernardi opera,* V, p. 239.

47. *In Dominica VI post Pentecosten,* 2, 4, p. 211.

48. *In Dedicatione,* 4, 3, ibid., pp. 384-85. Elsewhere *Sup. Cant.,* 28, 9-10. Bernard applies the words of Jesus "Do not touch me," "Noli me tangere," not to Magdalen, who is not named, but to every Christian. And he explains that it is by "the finger of faith, the hand of devotion, the embrace of desire" that Christ can be touched since he has been glorified.

49. In a hymnary of Fleury dating from the eleventh century, in the formula *O felix illa meretrix,* a copyist replaced the last word with *peccatrix:* D.-B. Gremont, "Le culte de Marie-Madeleine à Fleury," in *Etudes Ligériennes d'histoire et d'archéologie médiévales* (Auxerre 1975), pp. 203-26.

50. Pseudo-Hildebert, *Sermo 79, P.L.,* 171, 675.

51. *Sermo de S. Maria Magdalena, P.L.,* 144, 660.

52. Ibid., 665-66.

53. *In Cantica,* 33, 4, *P.L.,* 184, 173.

54. *Brevis commentatio in Cantica,* 9, *P.L.,* 184, 415.

55. Ibid., 3, 410.

56. *Meditatio in Passionem et Resurrectionem Domini,* n. 37, *P.L.,* 184, 765.

57. *Sermones LX-LXIV, P.L.,* 202, 822-39.

58. *Sermo LXII,* ibid., 832.

59. *Sermo LXIV,* ibid., 839.

60. *De institutione inclusarum,* 31, ed. C. Dumont, Paris (Sources chrétiennes, n. 76), 1961, pp. 124-26.

61. *Epistolae,* 169, *P.L.,* 211, 448.

62. *Dialogus miraculorum,* dist. VIII, c. 81, ed. Strange, II, p. 149.

63. Ibid., dist. VIII, c. 165.

64. Tubach, *Index,* p. 249.

65. *Exordium magnum Cisterciense sive narratio de initio Cisterciensis Ordinis,* dist. IV, c. 11, ed. B. Griesser (Rome 1961), p. 236.

66. The text is edited in *P.L.*, 112, 1431–1508, and restituted to the "milieu claravallien" by V. Saxer, "La 'Vie de Ste. Marie-Madeleine' attribuée au Pseudo-Raban Maur, oeuvre claravallienne du XIIᵉ siècle," in *Mélanges S. Bernard* (Dijon 1954), pp. 408–21.
67. *Vita B. Mariae Magdalenae*, 33, *P.L.*, 112, 1486.
68. Ibid., 32, 1485.
69. Ibid., 45, 1502.
70. Ibid., 29, 1479.
71. Ibid., 35, 1490.
72. Ibid., 30, 1480.
73. J. Layard, "The Virgin Archetype," in *The Incest Taboo and the Virgin Archetype* (New York [Dunquin Series, 5] 1972), pp. 300–02.
74. D. Hill, "On the Use and Meaning of Hosea VI, 6, in Matthew's Gospel," in *New Testament Studies* 24 (77): 107–19.

Epilogue

1. For example A. Dumas reviewing E. Fuchs, *Le désir et la tendresse: Sources et histoire d'une éthique chrétienne de la sexualité et du mariage* (Geneva 1969), in *Supplément* 32 (1979): 412; a critical review of this work has been given by J. Javaux, in *Nouvelle revue théologique* 101 (1979): 920–21.
2. Examples in the work quoted in the following note, p. 39.
3. H. A. Kelly, *Love and Marriage in the Age of Chaucer* (Ithaca: Cornell University Press, 1975).
4. Ibid., p. 94.
5. Ibid., "Clandestine Marriage," pp. 161–76.
6. Ibid., "Matrimonial Sin and Virtuous Passion," pp. 243–85. Good account of Bernard of Clairvaux, pp. 305–13.
7. H. I. Marrou has pointed out texts in *L'idéal de la virginité et la condition sociale de la femme dans la civilisation antique*, in *La chasteté* (Coll. Problèmes de la religieuse aujourd'hui), (Paris 1953), pp. 46–47. In the article "Frau" of the *Realencyclopädie für Antike und Christentum*, (1972), K. Thraede had already stressed the importance of love—and consequently the dignity of woman—in ancient Greece, col. 206; he shows that "happy marriages" are proved by funeral inscriptions 200–07; he also shows that the idea of "spiritual marriage," that is, marriage without consummation, is already present in the third century of our era, p. 211.
8. J. Janssens, *Le relazione umane e religiose negli epitaphi cristiani di Roma anteriori al VII secolo* (Rome: Gregorian University, 1979).
9. C. Carletti, "Aspetti biometrici del matrimonio," in *Augustianum* 17 (1977): 41–51.
10. For example in an unpublished letter to the bishop of Pistoia which I hope to edit shortly.

11. On the "ambiguity" of marriage in the twelfth century and its progressive solution, mainly due to a clearer distinction between "engagement" and "marriage," see J. Gaudemet, *Sociétés et mariage* (Strasbourg 1980), pp. 140–45.

12. On the control exercised over the marriage of women, even peasant women, in England during the twelfth century, and even after Gratian and the decretals had laid down that the consent of the partners was sufficient, see E. Searle, "Seigneurial Control of Women's Marriage: the Antecedents and Function of Merchet in England" in *Past and Present* 82 (1978): 3–43, with bibliography relative to the twelfth and the thirteenth centuries. This study confirms the fact that we are not lacking in informational sources on the marriage of commoners, and perhaps especially of peasants, on account of landed properties.

13. F. Laudy, "The Song of Songs and the Garden of Eden," in *Journal of Biblical Literature* 98 (1979): 513–28.

14. To the witnesses quoted in *Monks and Love,* Ch. 1, we may add that of Peter of Roye, a contemporary of St. Bernard, who draws a contrast between the humble works of the monks of Clairvaux and their previous condition: "Alios episcopales, alios consulares, aliarumque dignitatum et multae scientiae viros illustres et iuvenes egregios audio extitisse" (*Inter epist. S. Bernardi*, 492, 9, *P.L.* 182, 711).

15. The case of Sibylla of Anjou, who became a nun after having had four and perhaps five husbands, is quoted by S. Gregory, "The Twelfth-Century Psalter Commentary in French for Laurette of Alsace," in *The Bible in the Middle Ages* (Louvain 1979), pp. 123–24.

16. This "Lorraine" translation is quoted with translations of texts of St. Gregory the Great as a "specimen of the prose literature issuing from what I would like to call the 'Wallon-Lorraine Bible Translation Society' ", by S. Gregory, ibid., p. 125; cf. ibid., p. 119. The translation of a sermon is published by A. Houry, "Traduction en oïl du deuxième Sermon de S. Bernard sur le Cantique des cantiques," in *Miscellanea codicologica F. Masai dicata. MCMLXXIX,* vol. 1 (Ghent 1979), pp. 273–78. The author announces there another study on the same translation to appear in *Mélanges J. Horrent.*

17. The fact is studied by E. J. Weinraub, *Chrétien's Jewish Grail. A New Investigation of the Imagery and Significance of Chrétien de Troyes's Grail Episode Based upon Medieval Hebraic Sources* (Chapel Hill 1976), pp. 79–87.

18. R. J. Cormier, "Sources for the Trojans' Tent-Fortress in the Roman d'Eneas," in *Studi Mediolatini e Volgari* 25 (1979): 86–92, with bibliography.

19. To the texts already cited we may add the "Crusade songs" of *Conon of Béthune* and of *Guyot de Dijon,* reproduced by J. Richard, *L'esprit de la croisade* (1969), pp. 121–24.

20. P. Matarasso, *The Redemption of Chivalry. A Study of the Questo del Saint Graal* (Geneva 1979): careful conclusions pp. 241 and 244.

21. P. Trible, *God and the Rhetoric of Sexuality* (Philadelphia 1978), pp. 144–65, *Love's Lyric Redeemed*, in connection with the Song of Songs.

22. Examples of a witness to this are the *Versus epithalamii* which I have published in *Analecta S. Ord. Cisterciensis* 7 (1951): 58–59, and which I hope to comment elsewhere; and a new redaction of the *De languore amoris* formerly attributed to Guerric of Igny and which I hope to edit as well.

23. *Sermons autographes, XCIII: Pour la fête de la Pentecôte*, ed. *Oeuvres de S. François de Sales* (Annecy 1897), 8: 121; in the same sense: *Sermons recueillis. XXXIX. Pour le IIIe Dimanche de l'Avent*, 9: 423; for each of these texts the references to the works of St. Bernard are indicated in the margin.

24. *Sermons recueillis. XLVI. Pour la fête de l'Annonciation*, X, 10: 42.

25. *Traité de l'amour de Dieu*, I. 9, 4: 51–52.

26. Ibid., p. 53. Numerous references to St. Bernard, especially in the texts on the kiss, are indicated ibid., *Table analytique* (Annecy 1964), 27: 23–24.

27. B. de Margerie, *La Trinité chrétienne dans l'histoire* (Paris 1975), pp. 262–65.

28. This has been pointed out by P. de Santis in *Aevum* 53 (1979): 389–93, reviewing the edition of the *Hymnarius Paraclitensis* by J. Szövérffy.

29. According to J. Szövérffy, " 'False' use of 'unfitting' Hymns: some ideas shared by Peter the Venerable, Peter Abelard and Heloïse," in *Revue bénédictine* 89 (1979): 187–99.

30. J. Bourin, *Très sage Heloïse: Roman* (Paris 1980), p. 19.

31. B. Bowden, *The Art of Courtly Copulation*, in *Medievalia et Humanistica, Studies in Medieval and Renaissance Culture* (Cambridge 1979), 9: 67–85.

32. R. Hissette, "André le Chapelain et la double vérité," in *Bulletin de philosophie médiévale* 21 (1979): 67.

33. Ibid.

34. R. Hissette, "Etienne Tempier et les menaces contre l'éthique chrétienne," ibid., p. 69.

35. *Summa de arte praedicatoria. Ad conjugales, P.L.*, 2110, 193.